PENGUIN BOOKS

LOOKING
for the
AFGHAN

Richard Loseby was born in Port Moresby, Papua
New Guinea, in 1963. He grew up in Sydney,
Australia, before settling in New Zealand with his
family. In his twenties he left for the United
Kingdom and used London as a departure point
to explore more distant places, often on foot,
including Turkey, Iraq, Iran (at the turbulent time
of Ayatollah Khomeini's death), Afghanistan (with
Hezbollah mujahedeen forces during the war),
Pakistan, China, Tibet, Mongolia, the USSR and
finally back to London where he wrote his first
book, *Blue is the Colour of Heaven*. Richard is
Creative Director of Lowe Advertising and is
married with two children.

PENGUIN BOOKS
Published by the Penguin Group
Penguin Books (NZ) Ltd, cnr Airborne and Rosedale Roads, Albany,
Auckland 1310, New Zealand
Penguin Books Ltd, 80 Strand, London, WC2R 0RL, England
Penguin Group (USA) Inc., 375 Hudson Street, New York, NY 10014, United States
Penguin Books Australia Ltd, 250 Camberwell Road, Camberwell,
Victoria 3124, Australia
Penguin Books Canada Ltd, 10 Alcorn Avenue, Toronto,
Ontario, Canada M4V 3B2
Penguin Books (South Africa) (Pty) Ltd, 24 Sturdee Avenue, Rosebank,
Johannesburg 2196, South Africa
Penguin Books India (P) Ltd, 11, Community Centre, Panchsheel Park,
New Delhi 110 017, India
Penguin Books Ltd, Registered Offices: 80 Strand, London, WC2R 0RL, England

First published by Penguin Books (NZ) Ltd, 2003
1 3 5 7 9 10 8 6 4 2

Designed and typeset by Egan-Reid Ltd
Printed in Australia by McPherson's Printing Group

ISBN 0 14 301883 3
A catalogue record for this book is available
from the National Library of New Zealand.

www.penguin.co.nz

LOOKING
for the
AFGHAN

RICHARD LOSEBY

PENGUIN BOOKS

To my mother

What saves a man is to take a step. Then another step. It is always the same step, but you have to take it.

Antoine de Saint-Exupéry

1

Outside the window of my temporary office in Seoul, flags of the soccer-playing world hung limply from their poles as the hot and humid city played host to the World Cup. Unfortunately, the reason for me being there was not to enjoy one of the planet's greatest sporting spectacles, but to help a local advertising agency win a US$10 million car account. There was a week to go before the pitch, precious little time, and so football had to take something of a back seat.

However, once the work was done and the pitch successfully completed, my colleagues and I were invited to watch Korea play a vital qualifying match against Germany. The atmosphere was tense, the pride of an emerging nation was at stake and there was not a single Korean to be found who wasn't wearing at least one item of red clothing.

All except for Yi, that is.

Yi was a well-groomed, suit-wearing man in his late thirties with a passion for flowers, not football. Though he waved his red bandana, admittedly without too much enthusiasm, and chanted the slogans in chorus with the others, I could tell his heart was elsewhere.

We sat next to each other and in between offside traps and curling free kicks he described for me the fields he yearned for. As an amateur botanist, they were not the sacred football grounds of Wembley or Old Trafford, but the dust-dry border between North and South Korea.

'You have been there?' he shouted over the noise of his countrymen.

'I'm afraid not,' I replied.

His expression of disapproval suggested I had just been to Rome and not visited the Colosseum. Truth be known, however, I would have loved to have ventured up there. Borders have always maintained a strange sort of fatal attraction for me; a love affair of sorts, a romantic indulgence with places that are notoriously secretive; just a line on a map but so much more on the actual ground.

In the past, I explained in my defence, I had crossed some of the roughest frontiers in the world, both legally and illegally, including Iran and Afghanistan during the war against the Russians. I had also been one of the first through the Berlin Wall as it was opened up by hefty men with pickaxes and sledge-hammers. On the other side, practically alone as the next man became wedged between the bars, I had witnessed the incredible contrast of this bright white, sniper-friendly East German wall, compared to its colourfully spray-painted opposite in the West. I took in the lurid green grass that grew over the machine-gun nests, the rolling razor wire that gleamed in the morning light, before a flood of lesser-sized people had poured through.

'Please,' I said finally to Yi, referring back to his own story. 'Tell me about it.'

Instead of a wasteland of barbed wire, dirt and dry brush, he described exquisite species of flowers and plants growing in no-man's-land that could not be picked or examined. He had been stationed on the demilitarised zone, or DMZ as it is called, during his long years of compulsory military training, standing watch for invaders from the North. But in reality his high-powered binoculars were straining to make out anything but a human invasion. With eyes widening, he said the flowers grew amongst the millions of mines and every spring was a parade of colour. Some species, he added, were extremely rare. Undisturbed, they had flourished in their nooks and crannies, but sadly the only way to view them was from a distance.

'One day there will be peace and I will join the de-mining crew, so that I can crawl my way to them.'

'What about advertising?' I asked him.

'What about it?' he said, as if I had just blurted out a rather stupid question.

'Will you give up your salary, your position in the company, to do all this?'

He didn't bother to even pause for consideration. He simply shrugged his shoulders and said, 'Of course.'

All of a sudden I gained a new-found respect for Yi, who up until now had been, I thought, just another Asian ad-man. His commitment to the things he loved reminded me to keep my own priorities in order, not to lose sight of that which is real and tangible. I had been working hard, perhaps too hard, and I remembered what this did to my father in the end. Now I had my own family to worry about; I was a dad to two adorable young ones and a husband to a beloved wife. An early exit because of stress was not going to be my fate. Then and there I decided to take a leaf out of the book of Yi. I leant forward and tapped him on the shoulder.

'Thank you,' I said.

'Why?'

'Because you've helped me to see something.'

'You are going to travel again, I think,' he said with a toothy grin.

'You have your flowers, I have friends I haven't seen in thirteen years, Afghan and Iranian friends I once shared a great deal with and regrettably, I don't know whether they are alive or dead. I think I need to find out, don't you, once and for all?'

There was a massive groan as an entire stadium watched a German mid-fielder send the perfect pass to the feet of a speeding striker.

'Afghanistan,' he whispered, lost in thought for a moment. His lips were moving and he seemed to be trying to remember something. Suddenly he sat upright and smiled.

'Have you ever seen the blue flowers known as *Besseya alpina*?' he asked.

The Korean goalkeeper dived but could do nothing to prevent the ball sliding into the back of the net. The crowd cried out in pain, faces buried in hands, dreams shattered.

'Yes,' I replied. 'Yes, I believe I have.'

2

The morning of my departure, I was booked to do a live interview on a national radio programme. At most, half the country would be listening and I was told the interviewer could be a tough nut at times. She had wrecked many a political career with her razor-sharp inquisitions and I only hoped she did not lump politicians and authors into the same basket.

The call from her producer came through to my home. He was surprisingly nice as he checked the sound levels at his end, then informed me I would be on straight after the book reading segment.

'Nervous?' he asked.

'Just a bit,' I replied, with a sort of spluttering honesty.

He chuckled and then added sympathetically, 'Can't be worse than where you're going.'

I pictured him at his tiny booth with its double-glazed window looking through to the main on-air studio. He would be arranging the next commercial break and feeding information through to the announcer. There would be old coffee cups and ashtrays overflowing. On the other hand, in precisely two hours I would be at the airport checking onto a flight to Perth, then Dubai, before finally landing late at night in Tehran, the bubbling hot-tub capital of Iran's Islamic Republic. It wasn't an ideal time to arrive.

Just then a woman's voice sounded in my ear.

'I have with me now Richard Loseby, author of *Blue is the Colour of Heaven*, the story of his fascinating journey through Afghanistan with the mujahedeen in 1989, and who is now returning to find . . .'

I tuned out. Not intentionally, but in the back garden I could suddenly see the neighbour's cat stalking our guinea pigs, Blackie and Harriet. I raced out with the phone still against my ear, grabbed a lemon from the tree and hurled it in the general direction of the offending creature. I missed, but the shock of exploding citrus against the garden wall was enough to send it packing. Sometimes the lives of your son's pets have to take precedence over publicity. Having said that, I almost missed the first question.

I think it was, 'Are you mad?'

My reply was a jumbled mess of thoughts and words that tried to explain how it was a case of perspective. I knew the terrain, the language, the people. To me, Afghanistan was a known quantity. That meant going there was more of a calculated risk than crazy. Slowly, however, as the interview progressed, I was able to put my thoughts in order and relax. Talking to this disembodied voice, who as it happens was charm itself, allowed me to state my objectives, my doubts, my hopes and fears – for my benefit as well as the station's listeners, including my wife on her way back from the shops in the car and my mother in her living room.

In the end it went very quickly. The twenty or so minutes were up and the interviewer was thanking me and wishing me luck. But she did have one final question.

'Do you feel lucky?' she asked.

I could hear the nation waiting. I thought I could hear my mother put down the book she was trying to read for the third time that morning. I thought I could hear my wife slow down for no apparent reason in the middle of the main street. I was going back to Afghanistan to find a needle in the haystack, and on top of that, I had no idea whether the needle still existed.

A one-word answer seemed to suffice.

'Always,' I said.

3

I n Tehran, on a night when tempers were frayed at the edges like old rope and the city's automotive-owning community was on a war footing with everyone and anything in their path, blood was bound to flow. I had no idea, however, that it would soon be mine.

I had been here before of course; this place called Revolution Square. I knew the layout and the way the footpaths are used by motorists as much as they are by pedestrians. I should have known to look left, right, then left again even before stepping onto a footpath. But the long flight had dulled my senses and slowed my reactions, and so it was, within a few short hours of having flown into Mehrabad airport with my small green canvas bag containing the meagre possessions I had allowed myself, that I met the full force of a motorbike. It was taking a short cut I would later find out, only that short cut was apparently through me.

I think it was the handlebar that did the damage, catapulting me headfirst into the doorway of a nearby bookshop. My face met with the doorframe and immediately I could tell it would be bad. The first slow drips of blood soon turned into a torrent and before long I was bent over watching a pool of my life force develop on the stone paving, trickling down into the cracks and merging with the earth beneath. I didn't know whether to make my way to the gutter and risk further assault, or to stay put and decorate the bookseller's entrance. I chose the latter and tried the nose pinch that I knew wouldn't work. Sure enough, the torrent turned into something more like a dam bursting, or a flash flood. It wasn't pretty, and the owner of the bookstore was inclined to agree.

'Ya'allah, what has happened?' he asked.

I tried to look up but it was impossible to do so without making an even bigger mess, so with my head down and bent over at right angles I told him as best I could. He was by now letting out a string of curses at the state of Tehran's traffic and having guessed I was a foreigner, muttering apologies for a guest being treated in such a way. He raced off and returned with a large roll of kitchen paper decorated with pink roses and proceeded to offer the sheets to me one by one. A bucket was also slipped under my nose to catch any remaining blood that seeped through the paper. Once the flow had reduced to a manageable trickle I was able to look my new-found friend in the face.

Ali was about fifty-something and wore a white, long-sleeved shirt and pale brown trousers done up with a black belt that only just contained his prodigious stomach. Most Iranians are slender, which may have more to do with the scarcity of food rather than genetics, but Ali was an exception to the rule. Clearly in Ali's life there was food aplenty.

He took me through to the back of his shop and sat me down in a bare wooden chair beside a vinyl-topped table on which was a copy of Omar Khayyam's *Rubaiyat* and an empty blue vase. Around its middle was a pattern that imitated those found at Persepolis, or Takht-i-Jamshid as it is called, the ancient capital of Assyria to the north of Shiraz.

'Has it stopped?' he asked.

I pulled the bloodied paper away and nothing more came out.

'You were lucky,' he said. 'You could have hit the window and gone through the glass.'

The thought of such an accident made me shudder. Hospitalised on my first day back in Iran and spending valuable time convalescing. It wasn't something I had planned for.

'I'll be all right,' I said, feeling my cheekbone for anything broken. 'Thank you for your help and I'm sorry about the mess on your doorstep.'

'Books and blood,' he chuckled, 'go hand in hand in Iran.'

He was talking of course about the times in Tehran's past when the ugly side of religion showed its face and the hard-liners meted out punishment to anyone who broke the rules, especially the booksellers on Revolution Avenue who dared to sell literature not sanctioned by the clergy.

'You are a tourist?' he asked.

'Not exactly,' I replied, not feeling particularly fond of his choice of noun.

Ali readied his old samovar for a glass of tea while I cleaned myself up and told him about the past, how I had travelled for three months through Iran in 1989 on a one-week transit visa. His eyebrows rose at the mention of Salman Rushdie, *The Satanic Verses* and the resulting *fatwa* that was handed down at that time by the then Supreme Leader of Iran and defender of the faith, Ayatollah Khomeini. I told him about my experiences at the Ayatollah's funeral and my time in the Caspian Sea, amongst the jungle-choked ruins of the Shah's champagne playgrounds. I described how I had later joined up with Afghan Hezbollah mujahedeen in Mashad, a holy city near the Afghan border, crossed over into Afghanistan in the dead of night aboard a captured Russian troop carrier, survived several months of fighting in and around Herat, then walked for thirty days across the mountains to Pakistan.

What really made him shake his head, however, was the news that I was here, now, to find some of the people I met back then; to find out, particularly in the case of the Afghans, what had happened to them since I walked off into the mountains – how they had fared in the early days of peace after their capture of Herat, and whether or not they had survived the Taliban. I also owned up and said I hadn't spoken to any of these people since this time, and that I was armed only with a phone number and the faded memory of Hezbollah's headquarters in the back-streets of Mashad.

'You will be disappointed I think,' he said gloomily. 'There are three things that could have happened to your friends in this time. Either they have left the country, because in the past few years it has become possible at least for Iranians to travel overseas. Or, they are in prison. Or they are dead.'

Ali was not what you'd call an optimist.

His unwavering belief in the worst things in life did not depress me, however. I knew what I was attempting could not be described as easy, but sitting at home wasn't going to procure any answers either, so the only course of action was to turn up and use traditional methods of investigation.

Despite Ali's protestations and predictions of failure, I drank the tea, examined his books and then bid him farewell before walking gingerly back to my hotel in nearby Ferdowsi Street. It was a small, slightly run-down establishment, but friendly nonetheless, which made it worth the five US dollars per night the man at the front desk was asking. I had a bed, a single bulb hanging from its wire in the centre of the room for light, a view down into an alleyway leading nowhere and a concrete floor bathroom with a drainage hole in the middle.

It didn't matter though, I was only expecting to be there for a few nights before catching the train to Mashad and besides, I'd had my fair share of work-related five-star hotels recently. The one-star Hafez Hotel wasn't going to kill me. In fact I liked the sense of nostalgia it provided, harking back to a time when places like the Hafez were home.

I laid out my things on the bed and delighted once more at how little there was. It made travelling a pleasure. To pick up one's belongings in a simple bag and sling it over the shoulder with zero effort – that is happiness. I had a pair of lightweight trousers that could be washed at night if necessary and dry in the morning, two long-sleeved shirts, a new 'old' stills camera – a Nikon F-801s that replaced my trusty Pentax Spotmatic whose light meter had finally given up the ghost, a tiny Sony Mini-DV digital video camera recommended by a film director friend, a pair of seasoned walking boots that had long since formed a close relationship with the shape of my feet, two pairs of socks, toothbrush, notebook, a bar of soap and an ordinary black belt into the back of which I had glued an extra-thin layer of leather to hide enough US cash for my time away.

There was one more thing. A piece of wrinkled paper, actually the back of a torn envelope, slightly discoloured and bearing a faint scrawl in Farsi across the middle. Once I had decided to make this journey, it had finally consented to reveal itself after years of hiding down the back of a bedside drawer.

Of course I recognised it almost immediately as the note a young Afghan named Nebi Mohandaspoor had passed to me on the morning of my departure from Herat. Nebi was one of Hezbollah's experienced fighters who had given me my Afghan name, Massoud, and who taught me the ways of war – how to avoid the mines and use the cover of bombed-out buildings to journey from one place to another. In time he had become a trusted friend, who on more than one occasion had saved me from a sticky end.

The message was pure and simple. Translated, it read: *Come back soon Massoud.*

Try as I might, I couldn't help but feel that thirteen years did not exactly fall neatly under the banner of 'soon'. I had no idea what had happened to him, but Nebi more than anyone else was the one person I hoped to find. I would gladly fail in every other aspect, if I could just be successful in this one.

4

At the National Carpet Museum to the north of the city, I was watching a group of chador-clad girls receiving a history lesson from their teacher. The topic, I'm sure, was a safe and secure one that fitted nicely within the confines of Islam. Namely, carpets which depicted victorious battles over heathen foe.

Only it wasn't these carpets that had attracted their attention. A group had got away and were standing in front of a large 17th-century rug from the Caucasus that told the story of Adam and Eve. Down at the bottom, standing a short distance apart under a large tree, were the first couple wearing nothing but a smile. Actually, a cloth covered Adam's manhood and Eve was modestly protected as well, but for the young girls in black this was fairly sultry stuff.

The teacher eventually hauled them back to the main group, but the word was obviously out that there was some juicy flesh tones to be had around the corner, and so periodically the girls would conveniently get lost and find their way back towards Adam.

Watching them made me forget for the moment that my first day in Tehran had ended in failure. The phone number I had brought with me belonging to an Iranian called Shahria proved to be out of date. No one had heard of him or his family. It was a dead end, and I was instantly reminded of Ali's doom-laden forecasts of the day before.

I had met Shahria on the bus to the Caspian Sea and he took me to stay with his parents at their holiday house by the beach. We drank home-made vodka and played Gin Rummy for small change, both activities being completely illegal and highly dangerous. Later, he also drove me to Khomeini's funeral and both of us were in awe of the drama that followed.

They were fascinating times and I would have liked to have met up with him again because he might also have been able to help me locate Hezbollah. But it was clearly not to be. Without a phone book and no directory assistance there was no way of finding him. I was discouraged because the first seeds of doubt were sown. The enormity of my task lay before me and the warning bells were already starting to brand this venture a foolhardy one. However, watching the girls made me realise that where there is a will there is a way. As they found new and more ingenious excuses for drifting away from their teacher, I told myself that my best hopes lay waiting nine hundred kilometres to the north-east in Mashad.

With that thought in mind, perhaps the best person to talk to next was not Ali the Pessimist. But walking back to my hotel as the setting sun made the dented and dilapidated yellow cabs of Tehran look positively photogenic, I happened past his doorway.

'*Salaam*, Richard,' he called out from within his shop.

Ali missed nothing and no one it seemed. His girth probably meant that a fast getaway in a crisis was impossible, and so an eagle eye had become a necessity.

'*Salaam, Ali. Khoobee?*' I replied. It was good to speak Farsi again, and even after just one day the old confidence was return-ing. Though not fluent, I was good enough to understand most things that were said. In fact, I understood more than some people gave me credit for, which of course had its advantages.

'*Che kar mikoneed?*' he said, asking me what I was up to.

'Just walking,' I replied with a shrug of resignation.

But then his eyes brightened and his thoughts turned to dinner. He invited me to join him for some good Iranian food at his brother's restaurant next door.

He closed up, making sure a portrait of the late Ayatollah Khomeini enjoyed a prominent and central position in his window display. He said he couldn't afford a proper burglar alarm, but the old Ayatollah's photograph still carried a lot of respect, even amongst the criminal fraternity apparently. I asked him if a portrait of the present Ayatollah, Khamanei, would have the same effect and he rocked back on his heels. According to Ali, its effect would probably be the opposite.

Here was the first indication that all was not well with the state of the Islamic Revolution, now in its twenty-third year. Without Khomeini at the helm, the father figure was gone from Iran's leadership, and there were rumours already surfacing of discontent amongst the masses, evident by the fact that the moderate, reform-seeking President Khatamei had been voted back into Parliament by a landslide, much to the dislike of the ultra-conservative clergy who ruled with absolute power from their ivory towers.

I tried to get something more out of Ali, but the delicious smells of meat and rice emanating from the kitchen were too much of a distraction and I let the matter rest for the time being.

The restaurant was little more than a narrow hallway that widened at the rear into a sizeable room with about twenty tables, each covered in a plastic tablecloth printed with pink flowers. Ali ushered me to a corner table at the far end, near the kitchen, which offered a good view of the hallway and any customers coming down it. Suddenly I had the distinct impression he was looking out for someone.

As he kept one eye on me and one eye on the doorway, Ali told me about the recent events that had led to a death sentence being handed down on the head of a noted university professor and decorated war veteran, Hashem Aghajari. In a speech the week before, Aghajari had questioned the legality of the mullahs' right to rule Iran. This of course was taken to be blasphemy, a slap in the face of the Prophet Mohammad, and the predictable response to hang the poor professor was not long in coming. Today, university students had been demonstrating across the road from the restaurant and Ali was predicting a riot.

'They will send in the dogs of course,' he whispered through a mouthful of rice. 'To knock some heads together and calm things down.'

'Dogs?' I asked.

'Not the four-legged kind. They call them "popular forces", but everyone knows those who make up the ranks of the Basij are no more than animals. They are fanatics with sticks and clubs who throw women from windows.'

His last statement rang a bell. In 1999, a student uprising had been put down by these hard-line militia and a female student had fallen to her death from one of the upper windows of the university. The domestic papers said it was a tragic accident, but without a doubt the general consensus was that she was pushed.

'When do you leave for Mashad?' he asked, pausing to lick his fingers.

'Tomorrow,' I replied.

'Good. That would be safer.'

Just then a young boy of about twelve years entered the restaurant and immediately Ali motioned him to come over. The table screeched across the floor as Ali pushed it back slightly so that he could reach into his trouser pocket and pull out a handful of 10,000 rial notes. With practised ease he counted out three of them and passed the money to the boy, who stood eyeing the empty dinner plates at our table. After a brief conversation the boy was dismissed.

'My son,' said Ali, gesturing with a nod of his head towards the retreating figure. 'A good boy but, sadly, his mother and I are divorced. She is very, very religious and I am not. It was a problem.'

Ali didn't say much after that. The failure of his marriage seemed to weigh heavily upon his mind as he slurped his tea and picked at his teeth with the end of a match. Finally he let out an enormous fart and then laughed like a guilty schoolboy. But the smile was short-lived.

'God,' he said. 'Sometimes I hate this life.'

5

The taxi ride to the train station was interesting to say the least.

'Prostitutes!' the driver yelled, waving a hand in the general direction of some women in the street. He then rubbed his thumb up against his forefinger and said, 'All of them are doing it for money.'

I looked again and noticed one of the women was carrying a baby while another had a bag containing what looked like schoolbooks. I felt sure he must be wrong.

'Me! Wrong about prostitutes? Never,' he said, poking a finger proudly in his chest. 'I have been with hundreds of them and I can tell.'

I didn't have to ask many questions. The information spilled out from his lips with hardly a pause for breath.

There were over a hundred and fifty thousand prostitutes in Iran. Most of them travelled to other towns and cities to work, to avoid being recognised by their own people. They had few places to go, no brothels as such, so according to my taxi driver they worked outside.

For example, a woman on her own under a streetlight was definitely on the make. Under a bridge, same thing. The baby apparently was a ruse, a ploy to fool the authorities if any stopped to question her.

It was hard to believe that in a place like Iran there would be so many willing to take such risks, but if the driver was right, the sex industry was not only operating, it was flourishing.

As I got out of the cab and paid him the money, he winked and pointed in the direction of the station.

'You will see,' he grinned, and with that he was gone.

The journey to Mashad is a long haul. Fourteen hours by train, although most of it is through the night. I found a seat with a group of businessmen heading home for the Friday break, and a nineteen-year-old engineering student called Jamal, whose black hair fell down into his eyes causing him to constantly flick back his head. Jamal spoke English fairly well and liked more than anything the music of Madonna. He sang a few bars of the song 'Erotica' to illustrate his point.

'Do you know any others?' I asked.

'No,' he replied with a shrug of his shoulders. 'I just like "Erotica".'

Despite his taste in music, I immediately took a great liking to Jamal. He was an ideal person to improve my Farsi with, but more than that, he was simply a nice guy, full of questions about what I was doing and where I had come from. It was the world beyond his television set and Internet portal that inspired Jamal more than anything. He had four years of study left, but I could tell at the end of that time the world of engineering would have to take a back seat to the world proper.

As the train rolled out of the station and on into the long Iranian night, we talked about everything, from my plans concerning Afghanistan to Osama bin Laden to Miles Davis, the latter being my feeble attempt to improve his musical inclinations. But while he was not ready to accept that a trumpet player could dethrone the queen of pop, he had no qualms in believing that the Al-Qaeda leader was very much still alive.

'Everyone knows it,' he announced with a frankness that was slightly unsettling. 'Bin Laden is in Yemen. He escaped the American bombing and they smuggled him out through Pakistan, then by boat to the port of Aden.'

This was a lot more detail than I had expected. I asked him

where he got his information from and he said it was just common knowledge in the street. However, on the street in Tehran, I had already heard people say Osama bin Laden had changed his name to 'Mike' and was driving a cab in downtown New York.

One thing was certain, Iranians loved a good story. Give them a rumour and you will have hard fact in half an hour. This was a country of conspiracy theorists and the more fantastic the tale the more likely it was to become accepted. However, this observation has to be tempered with the following proviso: in Iran, sometimes the fantastic, the unbelievable and the downright outrageous actually do happen.

It was about this time that two of the businessmen decided to take an interest in our conversation. Neither spoke a word of English, but I could understand them well enough as they peppered Jamal with questions about me: what did I think of Iran, what was my purpose in their country, my religion, what did I think of Iranian women and the all-covering black chador, etc. These were the same questions I had answered the last time I was in Iran, thirteen years previously. Although then I was younger and perhaps a little more eager to please. Now, as long as I wasn't talking to an armed member of the Revolutionary Guard, I didn't care what I said.

Regarding Iran I was frank but positive, because I genuinely did have a love for the country. I had crossed its salty deserts, ascended some of its peaks and journeyed along its Caspian coastline, and the mark these places had left on me was permanent. My religion was solved with a dismissive wave of the hand to say I wasn't Muslim. But in relation to the subject of women, I was a little less restrained. I saw the chador as a prison watched over by jealous men from centuries ago, who guarded their women as they did their cattle.

Naturally it didn't go down all that well.

One of the men argued the case, saying it was the word of God that ordered a woman to mask her beauty so that a man could better devote himself to worship.

I asked if the sight of men was a distraction to women, and in which case, why didn't he hide his hair and face. He scoffed at the notion and an impasse was reached.

Happily, the matter was resolved by a game of Gol yor Pooch.

Mr Religious found a small stone on the floor and took sides with Jamal. I was left with the non-communicative one, although his silent approach to life revealed itself to be a major advantage in this age-old Iranian game of bluff.

Jamal and Mr Religious placed their fists one on top of the other and dropped the stone into the topmost one. There was much wriggling of fingers to disguise which hand eventually held the stone before they separated and sat there, waiting for us to begin the process of elimination. Saying *Pooch* would mean we as a team thought a particular hand was empty. *Gol* was the equivalent of 'goal' and would only be uttered if there was no doubt in our minds as to which hand held the stone. However, young Jamal had the habit of grinning like the Cheshire Cat whenever he had it, and as a result we quickly came to match point, which served only to sour the mood of Mr Religious even further.

'Do you know,' he said, holding up the stone between thumb and forefinger before it disappeared within his fist, 'the *Bible* is fiction. How can Jesus be the son of God?'

I told him that he was being too literal, and not to take what was written in a book to be the absolute truth, no matter what.

'Perhaps,' I said, 'what the *Bible* means is that we are all the sons and daughters of God.'

'Ha!' he replied, making his point by jabbing a finger in the air. 'You see, you don't know for sure. But the *Koran* is truth and fact. There is no doubt.'

It was a pointless conversation, and one in which poor Jamal had to play the part of translator most of the time. He was stuck in the middle, next to his devout team member.

'I'm sorry Jamal, for dragging you into this.'

He looked up from his clenched hands, trying to play it cool.

'It's OK,' he replied with a smile.

I looked at the knuckles on his right hand and saw that they were white. It was clear he had the stone.

Much later, we put down the bunks and I climbed under my blanket, knowing that sleep would come easily. The gentle rocking of the carriage and rhythmic clatter of the track below would soon work in tandem to their soporific best. I listened for a while, translating this sound into words for my own amusement: *Badah daram, badah daram, badah daram.* The train was talking to me in its own language, understood only by the lone nocturnal traveller.

Outside, a sickle moon on its back hung low in the sky, barely lighting the occasional village that swept past the window. I put a hand out and touched the glass, feeling through it the cold night air only millimetres away. Part of me longed to be free of the compartment so that I could put one foot in front of the other and walk to my next destination, feeling that cold air on my face not just my fingertips. But time was a constant foe on this journey. Unlike the occasion of my last passage through these parts when time was invisible, I now had a very noticeable deadline to contend with, a limit to the amount of time I could spend looking for Nebi and the others, before the bell for my return would sound.

And of course I had other responsibilities as well. Not just work but most importantly, family.

The little ones didn't really understand what their father was doing. I had been away on business for the odd week here and there over the years, but a month is a long time in a child's mind. It is an eternity of days and nights spent wondering when, and indeed if, that person will return. They would have woken and found me gone, unaware of the time I had spent sitting at the end of each of their beds as they slept, quietly telling them all would be well. I had written a letter for both of them, so that they might have something of me to hold onto, something that would ease their doubt if ever doubt came calling. After all, it is hardest for the ones left behind, and I knew well that feeling of loneliness. My own father had left one day and never returned, losing his life to a cancer that destroyed our special relationship.

Before sleep came to take me, I recalled the last time I saw him. He was very sick and what the cancer hadn't taken from him, the drugs to quell the pain were finishing off. My mother had called me in to hold him while she went next door to get help.

I found him sitting in a chair, bare-chested and facing a mirror his eyes weren't able to see. So I stood behind him and rested a hand on each of his broad shoulders, all the time aware he and I were reflected in the same mirror, while on the dresser sat a colour snapshot of us at the beach in happier times. I wanted to say something that would make it all better, but no words would come. All I could do was simply stand there and wait until the sound of footsteps started coming along the garden path. I heard the front door open and a low male voice which I knew to be our neighbour, reassuring my mother. He was coming down the hall with her. They were almost outside the room and I was about to walk away when, for a split-second, I thought I felt a hand on mine, a gentle touch that was imbued with a strength I found utterly calming. But when I looked again, my father was still sitting motionless with his arms limply to his side. I let go and backed silently out of the room.

6

At sunrise the next day, my ears popped as we climbed up onto the dust-brown plains of Khorasan. The orange-brown mountains now visible to my left were gigantic reminders of the fact that I was not far from Afghanistan. It was a familiar scene, of dawn light and hidden valleys in the folds of the hills, slowly revealed as the sun ascended. Small villages came into view as well, their inhabitants already up and about to hook up their beasts of burden to the plough for a day in the fields. This was the month of September, late summer or early autumn for this part of the world, so the last of the wheat was being threshed and the chaff separated, readying the grain for either storage or for sale at the market. Shepherds, usually small boys with sticks, were herding their flocks out of the corrals to where grass might be found bordering a mountain stream.

Once I saw an elderly man squatting in the dust, trousers down around his ankles, but not unduly worried by my face at the window. I think he even smiled. Either that or he was straining to make his bowels work.

Jamal was up too, and I met him in the corridor as I stretched away the night.

'Did you sleep well?' he asked politely.

'I always sleep soundly on trains,' I said. 'I think my body prefers to be on the move.'

He smiled and looked out the window at the lines of telegraph poles that flashed past.

'It must be fun,' he said wistfully. 'But Afghanistan is a terrible place. Only terrible things will you find there.'

'Have you been?' I asked.

'Of course not,' he replied, with a mocking smile at such a ridiculous notion.

'Then how can you know?'

Our journey continued for the best part of the morning, until the sporadic villages became more frequent and the guards arrived to collect the sheets and pillows we had been presented with the night before. As was always the case, the train slowed to a crawl at regular intervals before reaching the outskirts of Mashad, passing the less salubrious neighbourhoods first, which were little more than shanty towns of mud-brick walls and roofs that boasted only the occasional television aerial or phone line. Usually the doors were made of recycled tin from old oil cans, pressed flat and hammered onto a wooden frame so that the manufacturer's label was still visible. There were doors like these in the villages of Afghanistan I had come across years ago, and I wondered whether the owners of these homes were in fact Afghan refugees. Was I looking at the houses of my friends, and if so, how on earth was I going to find them in all this urban sprawl? Despair came to sit fairly and squarely on my shoulders. It seemed an impossible task, and the thought occurred to me that I had perhaps underestimated the scale of my mission. Here I was, click-clacking my way into a city of several million people, in order to find just one, namely Nebi. If I was successful, it would be an incredible stroke of good fortune, a lottery-winning performance.

Eventually the golden dome of the shrine to Imam Reza came into view between the office buildings and trees that dotted the city, and I felt better for its presence. The shrine is one of the holiest of holies in the Shi'ite Muslim world, a place of devoted pilgrimage that swells the city's population many times over during the high season. Fortunately this was not the high season, but nonetheless I knew that finding a place to stay in Mashad would be difficult for a non-pilgrim. Jamal had already shrugged his shoulders to indicate his concern, but I told him not to worry.

'Something will happen,' I said to him. 'Something always does.'

We jumped down from the train and walked the short distance to the main station via an underground passageway that passed beneath the lines of metal tracks. It was just as I remembered, even down to the smell – of diesel fumes mostly, but something else as well. I couldn't work it out until the passageway ended with a flight of concrete stairs that caused everyone to bunch up as they climbed. It was the pungent smell of an unwashed humanity, fresh from a long journey.

Outside the station, which was a typically vast hall under a high roof that amplified the noise and commotion beneath it tenfold, I joined a group of pilgrims who were commandeering a taxi to the shrine complex. Jamal was heading in a different direction, but before he disappeared he gave me his cellphone number in case I needed his help. It was a significant gesture, because in the days to come his help would be timely.

Within minutes I was piling out of the taxi with the others at a busy roundabout called Felakeh Ab. At its centre was a large garden, around which the traffic flowed and the pedestrians walked, jumped, ran and dodged. It seemed the style of driving was no different from that in Tehran, although if anything it was on a slightly smaller scale. At least there were fewer vehicles on the footpaths, but it was still necessary to keep a lookout for the odd motorbike or speeding donkey.

While waiting to make contact with the Afghan mujahedeen in 1989 I had stayed nearby for several weeks at a place called the Saba Inn. It was in that direction I was headed now, leaving the pilgrims to take their first look at the shrine and to gaze in wonder at the sight which had brought them all this way. With a bit of luck I might be able to secure a room before the rush.

Happily, after all this time, the Saba Inn was exactly where I had left it. It was a tiny place, with a large sign above the door that still bore the same Persian script in blue type, while the words 'Saba Inn' were in red, although the 'S' was tilting slightly to one side. I poked my head through the glass door leading inside and again, it felt like home, even though the revolutionary posters depicting the events of 1979 were gone: Khomeini's return from exile in an Air France jet, the bloody takeover of the American Embassy, the foiled rescue attempt to free the US hostages. In their place in the tiny foyer was a simple

Defend the Faith-style portrait with the current Ayatollah's face peering sternly out from his ample beard.

I walked up the few tiled steps to the office and smiled at the middle-aged man behind the desk. Even in a sometimes hard-bitten place like Iran, a smile is worth a great deal. It rarely devalues like a currency and it can nearly always be relied upon to smooth the waters.

Unless of course, you happened to be this particular gentleman.

He regarded my smile and proffered greeting in his language like an insult. I asked him how he was and he grunted, still with the same fed-up look dominating his face. I explained to him that I had stayed at the Saba a long time ago and would very much like to enjoy its hospitality again.

Just then a host of black ravens, old women in their sullen chadors, came flying down the stairs to my left. They swept past me without a glance, all except the last one. She stopped at the office and began to berate the owner for something which I could not understand, such was the speed of her tongue. The owner bore this furious assault in the same manner he had treated me, with abject indifference. Finally she finished, and with a swoosh of her robes was off after the others, down the steps and out through the glass door onto the street.

I looked back at the owner. He put some papers in the top drawer of his desk and spoke:

'Are you Muslim?' he asked in Farsi.

'No,' I said, remembering that pretending to be one carried a death sentence.

'You are not here to make the pilgrimage?'

I shook my head again.

'But this inn is for pilgrims only, and only for those pilgrims who are related to martyrs from the war,' he said blankly.

I told him I understood completely, but my journey although not a pilgrimage, was still an important quest in God's name, and surely, Allah would bless him for his help. I also said that I would be no trouble.

He looked me up and down. I knew that I could have passed for an Iranian without much difficulty. My hair and beard were black, and my clothes not unlike those found on most men in the street. In fact, I probably looked more Iranian than some of the Iranians, who had taken to wearing V-necked pullovers with large diamond patterns on the front that I remembered as being one of the more forgettable aspects of life in the late seventies.

Finally he turned around and consulted a wooden board holding a line of room keys. The room numbers were written in Farsi above every hook and I immediately recognised my old room number.

'Thirty-six please,' I said.

After a few seconds of consideration he reached up and removed the key to that room.

'How many nights?' he asked.

'A week perhaps,' I replied.

He grunted and gave me a form to fill in which was completely in Farsi. When I pointed this out, he spent the next ten minutes looking for a copy in English. As it happened, there was one in the bottom drawer of his metal filing cabinet. It had clearly been lying there for a great many years, and the edges were nibbled away. I filled it in quickly and placed it on his desk. As I went up the stairs to the top floor, I felt it was entirely possible that my return was only the second time a foreigner had ever come to stay at the Saba Inn.

Walk up the steps, then to the back of the building past the other rooms with doors left ajar to let the air in, then towards the large windows looking west. Stop at the end opposite the communal bathroom. Turn left and there is the door. Put key in door and feel the click of the lock turning, turning, turning back the clock. The handle is stiff but opens with a pull and a push, like before. In all the years, one would think something might have changed, but this is Iran. Why change something that isn't broken? The door swings open onto a small room with a single bed, a plastic mat decorated with flowers on a floor covered thinly in cheap, plain, olive-green carpet, worn now in places where feet most often tread. To the right is the window that looks out towards the mountains that will later be home to a setting sun. To my wonderment the curtains are the same, still thin enough to float in the faintest breeze, and as I push open the window they do just that as a warm wind enters my room. It *is* my room. My room where I hatched such plans few would dream of. Where I once placed aside western clothes and adopted the turban and *shalwar camise* of an Afghan. From this room I left to walk down to the narrow alleyway near the train station to join the men of Hezbollah, and there to sneak over the border at night, all the while holding down a crate of rocket-propelled grenades that clinked and clunked violently in the back of our stolen Soviet transporter. From this room started the journey of a lifetime at the age of twenty-seven, through a civil war that raged around Herat, across mountains that pierced the sky with jagged knives of ancient rock, over desert lands that yielded no life, until the relative safety of Pakistan was reached after a month of walking. This is the room in which everything changed for me forever. And walking into it again is like being that young man once more, on the brink of something immense – like sitting on a pier and dangling one leg in the Pacific Ocean, with both eyes ever fixed on the horizon.

7

'No one knows what will happen to you.'

These were the last words said to me by a man called Jagtoran Azizullah Afzali, a leader of a mujahedeen group I was with and an ex-colonel in the Afghan army. He was a man of few words at the time, distracted as he was by the coming battle for the village of Korskack, which made this one sentence all the more alarming.

At the time it was in connection with the road ahead, the long walk to Pakistan that was approximately seven hundred kilometres distant. But now in hindsight, standing on the footpath outside the Saba Inn, I think it wasn't so much a warning as a statement of fact. Once you cross a certain threshold, once you step outside of your own comfort zone, there is a greater degree of unpredictability that in some creates concern, and in others, joy. I for one subscribe to the latter feeling. There is to me no greater sensation than knowing that what you expect to happen is the least likely event you will experience.

My goal now was to start the ball rolling. To begin the process of picking up old threads so that they might lead me in the one direction I wanted to take, that of finding Nebi. So my first port of call was the Serai Sayid, a carpet bazaar not far from where I was presently standing, in which I hoped to find the people like Ali Fa'Al and Vali Astaneh who helped me all those years ago. It seems strange, but after checking into my old room I had expected everything else to be the same as well.

Sadly, it was not.

When I found the entranceway to the Serai it was locked solid, and an elderly man mending shoes had set up what looked like a permanent work address on the doorstep. I stood back and examined the building. It looked empty, run-down, decrepit. My mood sunk. Of course, I reminded myself, what did I expect after so much time? That they would wait for me to return! I had wanted to believe it would be so, but here was stark reality rather than wishful thinking. Looking up into those dusty, clouded windows, I could almost hear the clatter of a business that was centuries old, as traders from Afghanistan and Turkmenistan would bring their carpets. And the arguments! What haggling! I had been entranced by the skill of the deal of these men. The way they feigned insult when a quoted price was too high, thereby breaking off the negotiation before one or other of the party would find a new way to begin again the debate. It was like watching the tide flow in and out as one side would get the upper hand, and then the other. Finally, either mutual agreement was reached and the price settled with a handshake, or both sides departed. But then, sure enough, the next day the trader would return, ready to haggle once more. It was relentless.

Ali Fa'Al was a master. I had met him in Shiraz and it was he who had invited me to Mashad. Ali occupied an office on the second floor, while Vali was at the top on the fourth. From each floor you could look down at the levels below, all the way to the bottom, which meant that everyone knew everyone else's business. The Serai Sayid was a community of nosey-parkers, plotting and sub-plotting their way to another deal.

But no more.

The windows were barred and broken, the door an entrance to an empty shell filled with nothing but memories.

I moved on. To keep my spirits up I treated myself to a glass of *shir muse*, which roughly means a banana milkshake, but the sweet drink failed to wipe away the feeling that I might have come a long way for nothing. I resolved to try and get in touch with Jamal by way of the cellphone number he'd given me. Jamal had told me during the train journey his university friends in Tehran had given him the English nickname of 'Lucky'. My hope was that he would be.

He answered the phone almost as if he had been frightened by its ring.

'Salaam Jamal, it is Richard.'

Immediately his voice changed, becoming more relaxed.

'Oh Richard. Salaam. How are you? Did you find a hotel?'

Happily I was able to tell him that all was well, but I wondered whether he would be interested in a little translation work. I had decided to find out what had happened to the Serai and I knew that Jamal would make a better detective, even though my Farsi was starting to return. He agreed and we decided to meet in the morning outside the Saba Inn.

So for the rest of the day I walked, noticing the things that had changed and those that had not. Firstly, the shrine complex had enlarged considerably, almost doubling in size it seemed. Large areas of what once were back streets surrounding the shrine had been reclaimed and in this space, gigantic new mosques were under construction. Several hectares on the other side of the street from the Saba Inn were either massive construction works, or would be soon. I met one old carpet *bazaari* who bemoaned the soon to be demolished carpet bazaar that had been his home for the past forty years. He had survived the rise and fall of kings and ayatollahs, but with a shrug of his shoulders he had resigned himself to this particular fate.

'It is the will of Allah,' he mumbled.

We had tea on his wine-red Bokhara rugs, leaning our backs against a pile of colourful Qashgai kilims which were piled knee-high at the back of his store. His face was older than his years I suspected and like many *bazaari*, he had a five-day growth of grey stubble instead of a beard and thick round glasses, presumably required because of decades spent in the dim light of the covered bazaar. There was nothing surprising about him. He was, in a way, a typical carpet dealer from Mashad. What was disconcerting was his real name. Not Mohammad or Abdul or Ahmad, but Peter.

'Peter who?' I asked in English.

'Mathews,' came the reply.

I took a cube of sugar and then remembered I didn't take sugar in my tea, but still, the action seemed to fill in the awkward silence.

I soon found myself talking to someone who many years ago had wandered into a post-World War Two Persia, fallen in love with the world of antique carpets and rugs, and had never left.

'Where are you from originally?' I asked, keen to hear the rest of his story.

'London,' he replied, sipping tea from his glass.

There was just the faintest trace of an accent, but I could tell he hadn't spoken English in a good long while.

'My home was destroyed in the war,' he explained sadly. 'I was stationed in Tunisia in '45, so after VE Day there wasn't much point in going back.'

From Tunisia he had journeyed east and eventually found himself near the city of Basra, in what was soon to become southern Iraq. After that it was a small hop, skip and jump into Iran where he had become enamoured with life in the city of Esfahan. The beauty of its mosques and open squares caused him to settle down and learn a new craft. Up until then, the workings of an army diesel engine was all he knew, but these were quickly put aside in favour of carpet knots and wefts. Having developed some skill as a repairer, he had once again packed his bags and headed north-east towards Mashad where he had stayed to this day, rarely venturing any further than Herat to buy from the local dealers.

'But that was a long time ago,' he said. 'Things have changed since then. Now the Afghan rugs come to me, although there are no old ones left.'

I asked him what Herat was like before the war and his reply was a single word that he drew out, so that it rolled off his tongue for what seemed like ages.

'Beautiful,' he said.

'I was in Herat in 1989. During the war,' I said. 'But of the beauty you refer to there wasn't much left.'

He sat more upright and he seemed to be looking at me more carefully.

'On which side?' he said slightly cautiously.

'With the mujahedeen, of course,' I replied.

This seemed to be agreeable to him, but still he had more questions regarding the hows and whys of my time there. For an old man, there was no doubting his mind was still pin-sharp.

To put him at ease, I told him my story.

When I was a young boy in Australia, my father had brought home a story of an Afghan he had met while working in a branch of the Bank of New South Wales. The Afghans had come to the outback with their camels to help build the railways. But my Afghan, with his leathery, nut-brown skin and exotic clothes and head-dress (that I later learned to call a turban), became something of a hero to me, as did Afghanistan itself assume mythic status. I was transfixed by maps that showed his homeland, surrounded by the pink countries of the Commonwealth. I read stories of battles and knew off by heart the British Army's tragic history at the Khyber Pass. Then, years later, my father died suddenly, only four days after my fourteenth birthday. I was numb from the loss, unable to cope with the utter finality of death.

But that wasn't all.

Shortly afterwards, the Soviet Army invaded Afghanistan and the two events became intrinsically linked. From that moment on, I began to believe that in one I would find the other. One day I would go to Afghanistan to find my father, who lived on in a mountainous realm, with the Afghan by his side.

Peter Mathews sat back against his rugs and cocked his head sideways.

'That is quite a story,' he said finally. 'You should write it down.'

I smiled and told him that *Blue is the Colour of Heaven* was a living, breathing entity on bookshelves in many countries around the world. It wasn't going to make me rich, but it made me happy.

'Good!' he said somewhat triumphantly. 'I am pleased to meet someone who is happy in his work. It is a gift. When I saw my first rug, it made me smile as well, probably for the first time since Hitler dropped that bomb.'

The 'bomb' was a V-1, a doodlebug, the world's first Cruise

missile, used in the later stages of the war to target mostly civilian areas. Thousands were launched across the British Channel, carrying two thousand pounds of high explosives each, one of which landed at the bottom of Peter Mathews' East End street. Both his parents were killed and his ninety-nine-year-old grandmother.

'One short of a telegram,' he said hoarsely, referring to the congratulations she might have received from the King.

Just then the silence was broken by a muffled bang of falling masonry. A mechanical digger was going to work on a row of houses behind the bazaar, no more then seventy metres away. I looked at the glass of tea at my feet. The vibration was sending ripples across its surface.

I noticed his hand was also shaking.

'Here they come again,' he said.

8

The clouds came up in the night, but by dawn it was clear and cool. The daytime temperature would not be uncomfortable, which would be a change from the stuffy heat of Tehran. I looked out from my window and already a man was climbing to the top of his crane above a building site behind the Inn. The crane looked old and unsafe. One part of the ladder was missing and he had to climb the actual superstructure for several metres to bridge the gap. But at the top, bathed in the early morning light, he stopped on a ledge to face the shrine and bowed his thanks to the Imam. It was a form of health insurance, Iranian style.

Later, I met up with Jamal on the street and we went for breakfast at a local *kebabi* who was grilling small sticks of chicken meat on the footpath, over a pile of hot ashes in a metal bowl. He was using his shoe to fan the flames, so we settled for bread and cheese, and a yoghurt called *must* which was brimming with healthy bacterial life.

'I am sorry your friends have gone,' said Jamal. 'Business can be difficult here in Mashad.'

'What about your father? What does he do?' I asked.

'He owns a construction company.'

I looked over the tops of the surrounding buildings and saw the cranes gathered together like ships' masts at a boatyard.

'Building the shrine?' I asked.

'No, those contracts were given to religiously approved

companies, owned by the friends and relatives of the man who runs the shrine.'

I would have thought this was sensitive material, perhaps not to be talked about too openly, but Jamal was not fazed. Here, obviously, nepotism decided the outcome of a deal.

'But there is enough work to go around at the moment,' he said, waving an arm out towards the street. 'Mashad is growing and it is all because of the pilgrims.'

'And who runs the shrine?' I asked.

'Tabbasi. Richest man in all Iran and a friend of Khomeini. His son is famous for being a rich kid. People say Tabbasi is next in line for President.'

We finished eating and walked down to talk to the old shoe repairer on the steps of the locked Serai. But after a short conversation it was revealed he knew little. The doors were shut several years ago and he had been on the doorstep since then. No one came or went, no word was ever heard about the past inhabitants.

I stepped back again and looked up at the building once more, hoping to spot something that would tell me what happened to Ali and Vali. The memory came back to me of an old woman sweeping the steps each morning with a hand-held brush made of twigs. I remembered how I would see her when I came out of the Saba Inn four doors down. Just beyond was the Park Hotel, a moderately-priced hotel with an awning that stretched out from the entrance across the footpath, downtown Manhattan-like in its blue and white stripes. The only thing missing was a doorman called Charlie and a row of parked limousines.

No matter how hard I looked, however, the building refused to reveal its secrets.

Jamal approached with a shrug. 'There is nothing here,' he said.

We walked gloomily up the road past the old Park Hotel which had been renamed Qods, and had gone only a few doors when a voice sprang out of nowhere.

'Excuse me sir,' it said in punctuated English. 'Can I interest you in some quality antique carpets?'

I stopped dead in my tracks and looked at the face that was

smiling at me, a thin, brown face framed with short dark hair tinged with grey. The eyes twinkled slightly more than normal and for a moment I thought I could smell hashish.

Jamal had grabbed my arm and was urging me forwards. I resisted.

'No, thank you,' I replied. 'But can you tell me what happened to the Serai Sayid. I used to know some people there, but now it has closed.'

With one arm out pointing down the road in the direction of the Serai, I watched as the smiling man's smile grew impossibly large. His eyes bulged with excitement and he began speaking rapidly in Farsi so that small beads of white spittle formed in the corner of his mouth and were shot out like bullets in my direction. Jamal had stopped pulling on my sleeve and was listening intently. Finally, the man changed back to English. They were words I would long remember.

'There is not the Serai Sayid! Please sir, here is the Serai Sayid. Here!'

His hand shot up to a sign in Persian script above the door he was standing in front of. I couldn't read it but it suddenly looked familiar. Then the doorway came into focus, a double wooden door of old, old wood set into a space between two shops. It was open and inside I could make out a short passage leading to a dimly lit interior.

My heart must have leapt into my throat because I couldn't swallow. It all came flooding back, the smells, the echoing voices – a library of memories collected during the intense weeks I'd spent in this place. All along I had been looking in the wrong place, the wrong side of the Park Hotel, and because I thought I was sure of the Serai's location, my eyes had been blind to other possibilities.

Within seconds I was walking over old footsteps again, into the cavernous interior with its multiple levels lined with glass-fronted stalls, piled high with rugs and *kilims* from all points of the compass.

'Do you know Vali Astaneh?' I asked, taking the steps two at a time as we trooped upstairs.

'My name is Reza and yes, Vali is a very dear friend of mine,' came the reply. 'He is not here this morning but he will be returning in the afternoon. I have a shop here with many nice carpets. You can wait for him there.'

I knew I was being thought of as a buyer, probably an ignorant one who might easily be parted from his money in exchange for a couple of cheap fakes, but the thrill of finding the Serai easily overcame these emotions.

On the second floor another man approached us. He looked older than Reza and was a little more tidily dressed, like a schoolteacher in his late forties. In his hand he carried a string of prayer beads and I learned his name was Ahmad. The two men had a quick discussion in low voices.

'And what about Ali Fa'Al?' I said.

'Ah ha!' said Reza. 'You know everyone. Ali is not here today but tomorrow, maybe tomorrow he comes.'

Reza was herding me towards his stall and the more I looked at him the more I recalled the very first person I had met at the Serai thirteen years ago. Back then, wandering the floors, I had been accosted by a man whose vocabulary belonged in the sixties and who had offered to sell me some 'good shit, man'. After the mention of drugs in a place like Iran, I had not been long in leaving him alone. But here he was, still going, and behaving more and more as if the 'good shit' was still flowing through his veins.

Jamal was concerned. He came close and whispered a few words of warning in my ear. These were not good men, he said. He had heard their conversations and was worried I was going to become a victim of a hustle. Of course he was right. That was exactly what Reza had in mind. Ahmad was interested in a cut too, possibly. But I was able to assure Jamal that, unlike an unsuspecting tourist, I was not walking into the lion's den. This *was* my den! So much time I had spent within these walls in the past, watching and waiting, trying to extract information from the Afghan traders as to the whereabouts of the mujahedeen in Mashad, that I had long ago learned the ways of the carpet dealer well enough not to be taken in by them.

Jamal, however, had to get home. I thanked him for his help and watched him retreat back down the stairs, fending off invitations to come and view 'the best carpets in Mashad'. I knew I would see him again. Already his nickname 'Lucky' had more than held true.

As it happened, trouble was brewing between my new-found friends. Ahmad and Reza were exchanging heated words and the atmosphere was that of two wild animals about to quarrel over a kill.

'Excuse me,' I said. 'But I'm not here to buy carpets.'

They both looked at me as if I had just told them there was no Father Christmas.

'I'm here to find some old friends. That's all.'

There was a short silence after which Reza made a half-hearted attempt at guiding me to his stall at the back of the Serai.

'What about a small prayer rug? Very old, my friend, very easy to roll up into your sleeping bag.'

'No thanks, I don't have a sleeping bag.'

'A salt bag then? It will weigh nothing at the bottom of your backpack.'

'I don't have a backpack.'

'You are a tourist and you don't have a backpack?'

'I'm not a tourist.'

This clearly was a problem. I didn't fit the mould. Reza was starting to lose interest and I heard him ask Ahmad who I was. I replied before Ahmad had a chance to say anything.

'*Nevesandeh hastam,*' I said, which really put the cat amongst the pigeons. Telling them I was a writer was one thing. Saying it in Farsi was quite another. I could see they were worried I had been listening in to all their conversations. Unsurprisingly, Reza remembered he had to be somewhere else and with a mutter or two was off down the stairs. Ahmad watched him go and shook his head.

'Poor Reza,' he said. 'He is talking shit today.'

I discovered that Ahmad was Vali's business partner in his spare time. At other times he was a tourist guide and an English teacher. The tourist guide job had a symbiotic relationship with his carpet-selling exploits. Meeting tourists meant he was able to win their trust and lead them to Vali, who then took over the job of flogging them a carpet or two, sometimes more. He was one half of a tag team that wrestled money off the unwary.

I was surprised by his candour more than anything. Ahmad

43

was fully prepared to spill the beans, especially when we left the Serai and walked to a nearby mosque in the back streets away from the shrine. Gonbad-i-Sabz was the tomb of Mohammad Momen, a 14th-century scholar and physician, situated in the middle of a roundabout with a greenish turquoise-tiled roof that gleamed in the light. We found a bench to sit on and a place to talk. Such was his willingness to do so, it seemed I played the role of psychiatrist and Ahmad was my patient.

'I hate this fucking job,' he said.

'Why?'

'Because I have to do these things that I do not like doing.'

'What things?'

'Selling to foreigners. We call it "cooking the tourist". I have been twenty years in the kitchen, cooking.'

Just then a car tooted its horn as it drove by and a man waved out the window. Ahmad smiled and waved back.

'You see, that man is the chief of all the cooks. He is very good, the first in Mashad I think. The tourists like him, they trust him. He takes them to the historic places for free, and then after that, they buy carpets from him. Two hundred dollars in US currency they pay for a ten-dollar carpet. Sometimes four hundred. I have seen him working. He is a really good cook.'

We laughed. There was a funny side to this therapy and it seemed to be doing Ahmad a power of good. He was really warming up now and I started taking notes, with his permission.

'When I started this business, it was a different Iran. The 1970s when the Shah was in control. But the people got sick of him and they wanted him gone. However, we have this expression. We were like a fish in water – he doesn't know how useful the water is until you take him out.'

'Then came Khomeini.'

'Yes. But Khomeini was good. People still, to this day, love Khomeini. But he was surrounded by powerful people who wouldn't let him move. Do you know, Khomeini never once came to Mashad. Mashad, the holy city of Shi'ites and the Ayatollah of Shiadom never comes! Crazy! And all because Rafsanjani kept him in Jamaran, his palace in North Tehran, with stories of assassins waiting to take his life.

'Then there was the war with Iraq. My God, the lies the mullahs told. The young soldiers were sent into battle believing in the nine virgins waiting for them in paradise. They were even given a paste, you know, for shaving the whole body – down between the legs, everywhere, so that they would be clean in paradise. Clean for fucking their virgins.

'Even the Iraqis could not believe the lies. They knew the mullahs in Iran were telling our troops that victory would be theirs because the Twelfth Imam, Mahdi, was going to appear. Shi'ites believe the Twelfth Imam wears a green turban and rides a white horse, so the mullahs get actors to dress up like this and ride onto a hill, or something like that, near a battle. "Look, there he is – we will win, we will win! Now go!" they would say. But the actors were often captured by the Iraqi army and they would taunt our soldiers with megaphones: "We have three of your Twelfth Imams. How many more can there be?"'

'Religion is very powerful,' I said.

'Only in the wrong hands. Now all people hate the mullahs. They call them "British" because they believe MI6 trained them and brought them here. We also have another name, Sheikh Rubah, it means Mullah Fox. Once there were only 60,000 in Iran, now there are three million, and they have special free universities, free apartments, free laundry. My daughter pays to go to university. A mullah is paid to go to a mullah university, that's why there are so many. They do nothing and they get paid for doing it!'

He was laughing, but with Ahmad it was difficult to tell if he wasn't also crying at the same time.

'And then,' he says finally. 'My daughter comes home and I say, "What's this on your chin?" She has white hairs growing there and she says, "Baba! They put it in the water. It makes us lazy."

'You see,' he said, 'they add *Karfur* to the food and water. It is a drug to stop the young ones thinking about sex and to keep them docile.'

His voice was straining now with rage. Perhaps it was timely that once more we heard a car horn and the chief 'cook' drove by in the opposite direction. Ahmad was momentarily distracted and he waved back again, smiling for real this time.

'There he goes. That man is a fucking bastard. God I love him.'

I laughed. There were two people in the back seat. The girl was wearing a headscarf and the young man had blond hair. Two tourists, ready for the oven.

9

That night, the man behind the desk at the Saba Inn is telling me to go. There has been a complaint and I cannot stay any longer. He reminds me that this is a place for the family of the martyred, and clearly to some of those staying here, I am not in this privileged group. He is holding out my belongings which he has already packed, and my passport.

I argue of course. I stand there and berate him, not because I think it will help change his mind, but because I am being chucked unceremoniously out of my home for no real reason and damn it, I refuse to go quietly.

He tells me I am a foreigner with money, that I can afford to stay at the Qods Hotel, unlike his other guests who are poor.

The fire in me goes out as quickly as it had started. He is right. I am not the twenty-seven-year-old traveller with the dollar-a-day budget any more. I am not wealthy by any standards, but I have a nice car back at home, a house that is worth more than one hundred Iranian houses, and I think nothing of spending an amount of money on a bottle of champagne that would feed a family of four here for a week or two. So what right have I to claim a room in the poor-house? None it seems.

So then and there it happens. The empty realisation that the bars are on the window and Peter Pan has to fly away. No matter how you retrace your steps, you cannot turn back time.

I walk up the road to the Qods and pay ten bucks for a room at the back. It has a nicer bed that doesn't bear the imprint of the previous guest, and it even has satellite television. I flick onto BBC World and watch a documentary; oddly enough, about Iran's Ayatollah Khomeini. They are showing the masses at his funeral and I am astonished to see footage of the water trucks spraying water onto the crowds. Not because this is a crazy thing to do, but because I was there at that very moment in time in the year 1989.

Taking pictures.

From the top of a water truck.

It is no more than a flash, but for the briefest of moments I think I can see me. And what do I do? I do what any man would do if he caught sight of his younger self.

I wave.

10

Jamal was the first to find the offices of Hezbollah. Not because he knew where to look; on the contrary, he didn't know they even existed in his own town. But on the way back home in a taxi, the driver had been forced by the traffic to use a back street and Jamal had seen a hand-painted sign outside a large building announcing the upcoming Hezbollah reunion party.

'It was in big green letters on a white sheet hanging from a balcony,' he said excitedly on the phone.

'You're sure? Near the train station?'

'About two blocks,' he replied. 'I'll show you.'

There is no easy way of walking into a place like the head-quarters of Hezbollah. The building itself appeared to be fairly ordinary. There was a gate about the width of a car that proceeded through to an arched tunnel, that in turn opened out into a wide, uncovered courtyard. But all that ordinariness seemed to evaporate when you remembered this was the stronghold of one of the most notorious religious groups in the entire world.

Once upon a time, I had sat opposite its unremarkable entrance wondering whether I was doing the right thing. It was a sunny day. I could turn away, I had told myself, and surrender those fanciful notions of entering Afghanistan in the middle of a war. It would have been easy just to pick myself up and leave. But back then I had come a great distance over many months and I wasn't about to give up. I had crossed the road and walked inside.

Now, in the exact same spot, I was looking down the barrel of a different sense of growing panic. Having come so far again, after a long absence, I was worried that I would find nothing but a sad conclusion, an un-fairytale ending in which my friends were dead. Or what if they had joined the Taliban and were languishing in a Cuban jail? Or were simply untraceable?

I was still thinking about the possibilities as I made my way down the tunnel and came out the other side into the bright sunshine again.

An older man sitting on a chair in the sun got slowly to his feet as I approached. I held out my hand.

'*Salaam aleikum*,' I said.

'*Aleikum salaam*,' was the reply.

More pleasantries were exchanged before I got down to the questions I had come so far to have answered. I asked him about Nebi and he nodded, then shook his head, wiping a hand over his brow. There was no one here by that name. I received the same reaction to Nasur and Karim. It was hot in the courtyard and I could feel a bead of sweat running down my back. Like a gambler I was down to my last roll of the dice. I asked him if he knew the Commandant Haji Qarry Ahmad Ali, and immediately his face lit up with a beam of acknowledgement.

'Yes, yes,' he exclaimed. 'But Haji Qarry is not here today. Tomorrow.'

It was like a foot in the door to the eager salesman peddling the *Encyclopaedia Britannica*. I breathed a sigh of relief just as a voice from upstairs asked what was happening. I looked up to see a tall man in his late thirties wearing brown suit trousers and a white-collar shirt. He was leaning with one hand on the railing while he shielded his eyes from the glare with the other.

'Baba Khan,' called the old man. 'There is a foreigner who is asking for Haji Qarry.'

'What does he want?'

'I do not know.'

I intervened and explained that I was a friend of Hezbollah who had last been here in the year 1468 (which is according to the Islamic calendar that recognises the birth of Mohammad as the starting point of all things). As introductions go it wasn't much, but Jamal I noticed was still standing on the other side of the road watching, and so for the moment at least I was going to be doing all the talking. A long time ago I learned to keep conversation simple and the technique seemed still to be working. The man called Baba Khan was coming down the steps slowly, his eyes still adjusting to the light. He walked up to me and squinted. I suppose, I expected more, but in the end, all I got in reply was, 'I know you.'

11

Moments later I was sitting on a wooden chair in a bare office. The only other furnishings were a gun-grey metal filing cabinet with pictures of Khomeini and Khamanei stuck to the front of each of its two sliding drawers, past and present ayatollahs; a heavy wooden desk with an antiquated phone perched in the upper right-hand corner; and on the wall a framed poster of Khamanei again, Supreme Leader of the Islamic Republic of Iran, staring down on us with a stern, reproachful look.

It was the same room I had sat in the first time I came to Hezbollah. The exact same room I had waited in to hear the verdict of my request to be taken into Afghanistan. And the same room I had exited in a hurry, chasing a flying Nebi down the stairs, trying to put my boots on and not bothering with the laces, as a car waited outside to take us to war.

Baba Khan was the manager of Hezbollah. He sat forward on the edge of the desk with his hands clasped together on his knee, looking at me as I looked at him, trying to piece together the who, what and where of our respective faces.

I remembered him as a slightly gangly kid with a wispy moustache and a machine-gun. He had been at the mud-brick fort known as Mussa Abad, just over the border in Afghanistan, which had been the first staging post in the long journey to the outskirts of Herat. There was not much else I could recall, just a memory of him being in the background a lot of the time.

'Green tea or black?' he said finally.

It was still early in the morning. Black tea was normally reserved for later in the day, but I knew I was being offered a choice because I was a guest.

'Green,' I replied.

He got up and in two strides was through the diaphanous curtain across the doorway, slipping on his shoes as he went. The backs were bent down and flat after years of being worn like slippers, with the laces tied in a permanent knot.

Outside, down on the pavement, I could see no sign of Jamal.

Baba Khan returned with a chair which he placed opposite mine. He sat down and ran a hand through his hair, then smiled at me as if he were thinking of something to say.

'May you not be tired and may you have long life,' I mumbled, holding a hand to my heart in the Muslim fashion.

'Praise be to God,' he added, having returned the blessing.

We sat in further silence until the curtain was again whipped back and another man entered with a metal tray bearing three glasses of *chai sabze*. There were more greetings and I accepted the proffered glass. It was incredibly hot and I was able to hold it only for a few seconds before being forced to place it hurriedly on the floor. Baba Khan, I noticed, was still holding his glass by his fingertips. Slowly he raised it up to his lips and blew the steam away before taking a sip.

'We thought you were dead,' he said at last in Farsi, sliding a finger across his throat in a single motion.

'Who?' I said.

'You,' he said.

'Me?'

The words flew like bullets across the room, ricocheting against the walls and floor. A smile creased his face and I began to laugh as well.

'After you left Herat,' he continued, 'we were told that a foreigner had been captured and killed up in the mountains. It made us very sad, but we prayed it wasn't true. Then, when no one heard anything more from you, we began to believe you were dead.'

I listened to this as one would to an account of one's own death, with a mixture of awe and embarrassment. I reprimanded myself for not trying harder to send news of my safe journey across the country. I owed them this much, and yet I had failed in my duty. A guest has a responsibility to his hosts.

'I am sorry,' I said.

Just then, the curtain over the door was drawn back an inch or two and one half of a large face peered through. Shoes were slipped off and the large face soon gave way to an even larger frame that took up the full width of the doorway. The newcomer was wearing a long dark turban and the customary *shalwar camise* of an Afghan.

Immediately Baba Khan got to his feet and I soon followed, taking the thick, meaty hand of the man and greeting him accordingly. Another chair was produced and with a heavy exhalation of breath he sat down, taking the loose end of his turban and letting it fall across his lap.

I looked at him closely and once more felt a growing sense of recollection. Time can do a lot to change a face. Hair will thin and turn grey. Young backs become more rounded, as if age bore with it a weight of years. But this face I knew. It once belonged to a man called Ali who was a famed fighter and a feared opponent in the wrestling ring. In Herat, in between the shooting, he would casually pick up young recruits to Hezbollah and in a few quick moves have them begging for mercy, their bones creaking under the strain of being bent at unnatural angles. It was his own brand of initiation into the harsh realities of war.

Baba Khan pointed at the large figure now eyeing me with some interest.

'Do you remember him?' he asked.

I nodded enthusiastically.

'Of course. Ali is famous.'

Ali, however, was looking slightly perplexed. He spoke in a low voice to Baba Khan who then filled him in on the details of who I was. Within seconds I was back on my feet, placed there by Ali who kindly straightened my spine with a hug of bear-like proportions. He then kissed me on both cheeks.

'Massoud!' he roared.

We both sat back down and continued to smile at each other, as he and Baba Khan rapidly exchanged words of incredulity.

54

With me, however, Ali used simple words and said them slowly, as is the way when some people talk with foreigners.

'Dead!' he said, pointing a finger at my chest. 'You!' Then he raised both his hands, palms up in a questioning manner.

I happily started in on the tale, knowing that it would be repeated a hundred times more in the weeks to come. My journey after leaving Herat was listened to in silence, and my account of the walk through the mountains and my eventual arrival at the Pakistan border near Kandahar without a visa. Then of being smuggled across the line in the back of a gaudily painted Pakistani jeep, followed by my later deportation from Pakistan into China and then the long haul home to London aboard the Trans-Siberian Railway.

In the end there was a round of polite applause and a slap on the shoulder from Ali that almost knocked me sideways. What impressed him most was that I apparently hadn't changed. He put a hand to his own weather-beaten face and stroked his greying beard, then he pointed to me and wondered at how young I was in comparison. I told him life had been kinder to me than to him. I had not spent the last decade or so in Iran and Afghanistan.

'True,' he said. 'Life is very hard here.'

All that morning and for part of the afternoon I was introduced to new friends and old. Some would say nothing and just sit and watch, bewildered by this stranger in their midst, all the while hearing stories about him in connection with Hezbollah. I was like a long-lost relative, finally returning to the family.

But one face that didn't appear was that of the man I most wanted to meet. I was in fear of asking the question, in case there was bad news. But even so, by the afternoon, I could not bear not knowing any longer.

'Baba Khan,' I said. 'What happened to Nebi? Nebi Mohandaspoor?'

You could have cut the air with a knife. People stopped and stared. Someone who was hard of hearing asked what I had said.

'Nebi was in an accident, Massoud. A mine. There were many *shayeed*.'

The feeling of dread that came over me was like a lead

weight, dragging down any hope I had left. *Shayeed* means martyred, and there are no living martyrs. Martyrs are dead people.

'When?' I asked.

There was some consultation and an approximate date was agreed upon.

'1468,' replied Baba Khan.

1468 was the year I was in Afghanistan. 1468 was 1989 in our calendar.

'I was there that year,' I said.

Further consultation ensued and heads nodded in unison. One old man in the corner whom I hadn't seen come in was more animated than the others.

'That is correct,' said Baba Khan, before indicating the old man. 'Haji Basheer remembers. The accident was a few weeks after you left.'

The enormity of this news left me speechless. I pictured in my mind's eye the last time I had seen Nebi, the morning of my departure from Herat. I saw his face and felt again the warmth of our final embrace, like two brothers at a crossroads. I had never known anyone like him, nor would I ever possibly again.

Staying a minute longer was impossible. The desperate need to escape was now overwhelming. It's an old reaction, born out of the shock of finding out my father would not last the night, when all week I had been planning the fun we would have on his return to health. And so I had to get out. The urgency of my departure was probably not entirely polite, but nonetheless I made an excuse, shook the hand of all those in the room and then made for the door. The room was suddenly hot and airless, like I imagined a coffin to be.

12

The next day was cloudy and definitely cooler. Leaves had started to fall and fill the open drains that lined the road. The sweepers with their giant brooms waged a hopeless battle against autumn, but at least they had a job, which was not always the case. Beggars, some with horrible injuries, had to find other means of survival. One man had what looked like elephantiasis. His head was three times normal size and covered with the worst boils I had ever seen. He dabbed at them with a white handkerchief and I had to turn away at the sight of yellow pus.

Another man appeared to be the victim of a mine. The lower part of his left leg was missing, leaving a rough stump that shook violently and uncontrollably from severe nerve damage.

All of them faced a winter on the street, when temperatures would get down to below zero.

There was something about this that seemed to fit my mood. Mashad was a curious place. It could lift up your hopes and then just as easily dash them against the rocks. And so it was all the time, up and down, up and down, until mentally you felt like something small floating down a river, always at the beck and call of the greater power around you. A single day could feel like any other person's week or even fortnight, a veritable jumble of emotions. The only sure thing was that waiting around the corner would be yet another extreme.

And so it was that I met Vali again, my carpet-dealer friend from long ago who owned a stall at the Serai Sayid.

After eating a breakfast of bread and bright red tomatoes that dribbled their juices down my chin, I had walked back to the Serai. Inside I managed to avoid Reza and I sneaked up the flights of stairs to the topmost level. There, in the far corner, I found a wiry man in a grey flat cap that matched his grey waistcoat and trousers, busily going through an old diary. Vali always had a diary. It contained the names and addresses of people he had met through the years, people he had sold carpets to, people he hadn't sold carpets to but knew one day that he would, people from all over. Vali didn't need to travel and see the world any more. The world came to him and he recorded every encounter on the day that it happened, without fail. I knew that somewhere in one of his old diaries I would find myself.

'Hello, Vali.'

Full of energy as always, his head snapped up as he closed the book. There was a split-second's pause and then all hell broke loose.

'My friend! It is you!'

He leapt up and rushed over, one hand still on his book of names as we hugged and slapped each other on the back. I immediately felt better, better for having found him in one piece and in good health. He was grinning from ear to ear.

'They said a foreigner had come to see me, someone from a long time ago, but I didn't know who. Now I can see it is you.'

He stepped back and took a good look at me.

'Wow,' he said. 'You haven't changed.'

I took note of the obvious signs of old age in the colour of his hair and the lines on his face. His eyes, however, still had the same glint.

'Neither have you, Vali.'

I took a seat on a pile of rugs beneath a high window and watched Vali busily prepare his dented old samovar for a morning cup of *chai*. The bottom drawer of his desk revealed a small packet of what looked to be orange threads of cotton, although it was soon apparent they were not, as he pulled out a few strands and dropped them into a nearby teapot.

'Do you know what this is called?' he asked with glee. Then, not waiting for a reply, he answered his own question. 'We call it *zah faron*.'

I repeated the words a few times in my head until they became one. Only then did the penny finally drop.

'Saffron!' I exclaimed.

'Yes, yes. Very expensive all over the world. You can buy very good saffron in Mashad. If you need to buy some, I have a friend who can help you.'

The samovar began to whistle as I listened with quiet amusement. Vali always 'knew' someone when it came to buying or selling something. He was the eternal middleman who made a lot of his money by making a cut on every deal. But having said that, he was also there to make sure you were never ripped off. No one could ever accuse Vali of being dishonest, but for this reason he had also seemingly never made the big time in business either. Honesty is not a trait highly prized amongst Iranian business people.

'Do you still have those *kilims* I sold to you?' he asked.

Impressed with their wonderful colours and intricate deigns, I had bought several Kurdish flat-woven carpets the last time I was in Mashad. One was on the floor in my home, but the others I had sold in London years ago to help finance the writing of my last book. There was one that Vali had called 'the rug of a thousand kisses', a title he had almost certainly made up on the spot. However, it was beautiful and I was sorry to let it go. In the end, a wealthy English stockbroker friend had purchased it for his girlfriend. I told Vali this and he looked a little like a guilty schoolboy caught with his hand in the biscuit tin, so I knew my assumptions about the *kilim* were correct.

'What happened to your old partner?' I asked.

'Shahria is now in America. His brother is a very rich carpet dealer with many shops. They sell silk rugs for many thousands of dollars to the fat Americans.'

He laughed and stood upright, holding the teapot in one hand and rubbing his flat belly with the other.

'Man they eat so much,' he said. 'I saw a picture of this man once, who weighed over one thousand pounds. It took twenty men just to roll him over in bed!'

He poured the tea into two small glasses without spilling a drop.

'Twenty men!' he repeated incredulously, before suddenly growing silent as an idea started to form in his mind.

'What bed could stand such weight?' he mused. 'Truly, they must make strong beds in America.'

I nodded and sipped my tea. The aromatic flavours of the Orient filled my senses and I thought, if someone were to ask me, would I exchange this moment in Iran for another in the bloated land of fast food and French fries, I would say never. No. Never. The taste of the tea was good and refined. No fuss to create. No double-decaf nonsense, or special low-fat goat's milk. Just hot water and tea-leaves, with a few bits of a fragrant flower thrown in for a special occasion.

Sometimes we complicate things too much. But then of course, we can.

That night Vali invited me to his house for dinner. I met him at a bus stop near the holy shrine, just as the last light was fading from the evening sky and the stars were beginning to appear. The cars were bumper to bumper and there were more people than ever on the footpaths. Making headway was near impossible, so the only thing to do was walk along the road between the vehicles, keeping an eagle eye on any that might suddenly lurch forward for no apparent reason.

Vali was already there waiting, diary in hand. In between its pages he found a few crumpled-up bus tickets for the ride home. But first, he said, he wanted me to help him send an e-mail.

The diary flicked open again and he placed a finger on a page, pointing to a scribble of writing that looked as if a spider had dragged itself through a patch of ink and then crawled across the paper, bleeding black blood from every claw.

According to Vali it was the address of a man from Denmark whom he had entrusted with some carpets. The idea was that once the man reached his home he would forward a bank cheque to Vali in Mashad. It was now several months on and still no cheque.

I knew a Dane once. This particular Dane had cheated me

out of five quid in a pub quiz in London. I wasn't hopeful about Vali's chances.

'Can you make out this address?' he asked.

'I can give it a try.'

Down an alleyway beyond the bus stop we came to a glass door that opened into a long corridor lit with a single bare bulb in the ceiling. As we entered, it dimmed slightly for a few seconds, and then glowed brightly again.

Vali noticed this and said, 'Good. He is here.'

At the end of the corridor was a set of double doors, behind which was the source of the power drain. It was a room filled with computers and a dark-skinned man in a white long-sleeved shirt who was going from machine to machine, switching them on.

'*Salaam aleikum*,' said Vali in a way that was a touch more reverent than his usual manner and tone. He had even put his hand to his heart and bowed slightly from the hip. It was as if this was someone he wanted to curry favour with.

I followed suit and stuck out my hand as Vali introduced me. I heard him say the word for foreigner just as we shook hands, but it was plainly obvious the man who ran the computer shop did not want to come into direct contact with an infidel. He physically recoiled, both his hand and body, to a distance a good few feet away and then proceeded to eye me with something approaching disdain. I laughed, because these things I find funny rather than infuriating. In fact the more developed the sense of religious fanaticism in someone, the more likely I am to want to know what it is that makes them tick. So, much to the computer man's dismay, I asked him innumerable questions and delayed his departure for evening prayer, which put him in a right old state.

His name was Mohammad Ali and he was an Arab from Jordan whose dislike of things un-Islamic bordered on the obsessive. For this reason the western brand names of all his computers were removed by force, or scratched off and then replaced with a few pen lines of Arabic. The calendar above his desk by the entrance had a number of scenic photographs of Mecca and Medina, but also one of a lovely Orthodox Greek church on the island of Paros that he had deliberately cut out, leaving only its description at the bottom. There was one thing he would not be able to remove, however, and I contemplated telling him his own name had been taken by a black American boxer who was universally loved, but particularly in the good old United States of America. What stopped me was the fear that this would frustrate him to such a degree he might whip out a knife and kill himself on the spot. Not a bad thing, some would say, but I for one did not want the blood on my hands.

Surprisingly, his desire to get away from me increased so much he left for the local mosque without locking up. Instead, he asked Vali to do it once we had finished with the e-mail.

Unfortunately, the search for the Dane proved as unsuccessful as I had anticipated. None of the usual search engines coughed up anything useful, except for an article on the care and breeding of Great Danes. There was a picture of an owner who was as fat and round as the dog was tall; a smiling chubby face in shorts and singlet, kneeling down next to a faithful hound named Bernie.

'Americans,' muttered Vali, shaking his head in awe. 'Man, they eat so much.'

We left after that and made the rest of the journey by bus to Vali's house, which was an hour outside of the city in a new neighbourhood. It was so new, the local council hadn't got round to finishing the footpaths, and the mountains of earth and weeds proved a difficult obstacle to his front door. Once inside, however, it was as warm and inviting as any home.

A flurry of activity in the form of a young boy came hurtling round a corner to meet his father, but stopped short at the sight of me. Then a woman appeared briefly, without a headscarf, before she vanished back behind a kitchen door to gather herself for the visitor. His daughter also peaked into the room from the same doorway and then hid away.

Vali on the other hand was beaming.

'My family!' he said, gesturing proudly to the almost empty room.

His son stood there coyly, constantly shifting his weight from one foot to the other and looking slightly lost. Support came finally when Vali's wife and daughter reappeared and I was introduced to each in turn. His wife was lovely. She possessed a kind face that was older, however, than her thirty-something years, thanks no doubt to the considerable amount of time spent raising children and looking after her house and husband. She wore no make-up of course, though her dark eyes were large enough not to need any help of this kind. Her clothes meanwhile comprised many pretty layers of light and dark cloth so that they seemed to wrap her in a cocoon of contrasting colours, with only her face and one arm showing. The other arm was tucked within the folds of material, holding it all together from the inside.

The daughter was a younger version of her mother, but with pimply skin and buck teeth that unfortunately undid much of the beauty she had inherited. However, she had the most wonderful voice that spoke to me in simple English and welcomed me to their home. My boots duly deposited at the door, I was led to a place against the far wall on the floor and made comfortable with large pillows of old carpet on one side and faded *kilim* on the other. The main room, which was arranged in an L shape, was large and empty, save for these few pillows and a television set in the corner. Several layers of carpets covered the floor so that it was soft and spongy underneath.

The television was turned on for my benefit by Vali's son and I made a point of admiring the size of the set. At this, he raced off to his bedroom and seconds later loud music began to pound through the walls, competing against the sound coming from the television. Pink Floyd's 'Money' was fighting a convincing battle against the evening news. Vali held his hands to his ears like any father would and screwed up his eyes.

'Man, I hate this music,' he said.

His son was despatched and the music of Pink Floyd soon turned into Dr Zhivago's 'Somewhere my love'. It was musical comedy at its highest, although the television was eventually silenced when a plastic mat was spread out on the floor, signalling the fact that dinner was about to be served.

Over a meal of rice, chicken, unleavened bread and salad, Vali encouraged his children to practise their English, something which neither was very keen on doing. However, I was interested to discover what life was like for Iranian teenagers in the 21st century, and decided to grill my young friends. It was a surprise to find out that their lives were completely different.

Computer games were the stuff of dreams. Vali's son had only heard of such things as PlayStations, but couldn't tell me what one looked like or what it did. Videos were out of the question because no one had a video recorder, although apparently there was a rumour that someone in the street was thinking of buying a VCD player – a poor cousin to the DVD players that could now be found in most western living rooms.

'What about a girlfriend?' I asked the boy.

There were peals of laughter and much tittering behind female hands while Vali's son turned a bright beetroot colour. Vali spoke for him.

'My son is not yet engaged,' he said. 'Here it is different. Of course the boys and girls do not see each other until after the marriage.'

Vali reached over and rustled the young boy's hair affectionately.

'But one day soon, OK?' he added.

So here he was, no more than fifteen and already being lined up with a partner for life. It sounded cruel, but there was more to come. Shortly afterwards a friend of Vali's daughter came for the evening English lesson with Vali, who clearly made a little money on the side by teaching. Her name was Somaryeh and without doubt she was the most beautiful young woman I had ever seen. She wore very slight make-up and a perfume that teased the senses unfairly. But at seventeen years of age she was already married to a boy of twenty-two. In the lessons that followed, which were made up of Vali asking mostly personal questions of Somaryeh and his own children, I was able to glean even more information about her.

'What is your mother's name?' he asked, before repeating the question in rapid Farsi.

'Um, my name, um . . . my mother's name . . . is Sanaz,' she replied slowly.

'How old is she?'

'She is, um, forty . . . no, thirty years.'

My ears were suddenly pricked. A seventeen-year-old girl with a thirty-year-old mother can mean only one thing. Somaryeh's mother was just thirteen when she was born.

When the lessons were over and Vali and I were sipping hot tea alone, I asked him about this. His reply was straightforward.

'This is the way sometimes,' he said. 'The girl is married off very young and of course she will have children. The parents are always anxious that the girl should find a husband soon, before they are all taken. They do not want to be forced to marry her to an older man with one or two wives already.'

It was sad to think that Somaryeh, and other girls like her, would not be able to enjoy their youth before children came along to force adulthood upon them. Vali was not so sure.

'But her husband is a lucky man, I think,' he shook his hand in front of him and grinned mischievously. 'Very, very lucky indeed.'

Soon Vali was yawning and it was time to go. I thanked his family and walked with him back to the road to flag down a taxi in the darkness. It had been good to spend the time away from the news about Nebi. But now, waiting on the side of the road, the sadness of his death came back to haunt me. It was a long wait and there was no escaping the fact that it was getting colder by the day. The seasons were changing. Winter was fast approaching and it wouldn't be long before temperatures sank down into single digits, perhaps even further. However, more than that, there was a strange, almost imperceptible feeling in the air that all was not quite right with the world. It was as if something, somewhere was about to happen. And then, almost on cue, it did.

Vali nudged me gently.

'Do you feel that?'

I looked down at my feet but said nothing. It was there in the ground, the faintest sign that the earth was setting right what was wrong.

'Earthquake,' he whispered.

13

In the dream, I am walking across fields of harvested wheat again. The short crackle of dried wheat stalks is sounding underfoot, the stubs of which I can feel through the soles of my boots. Dust rises with each step and I see an ancient man, hobbling and grey, coming towards me through the heat haze. I ask him if he has seen Nebi, and he gestures silently along the trail as it winds through the field and up into a valley before disappearing over a distant ridge. Then he is laughing and I cannot understand why. But the laughter turns to music, a strangely familiar melody played on an unseen accordion that does not belong in this landscape. It is a cheerful, lilting tune more suited to the café society of Paris, a far cry from this Afghanistan.

I shelter my eyes from the glare of the sun and look back the way I have come. There are many miles behind me, so many in fact that when I try to remember where this journey began, a picture of it fails to appear. It is tantalisingly close but forever distant, like smoke from a passing ship that lies just over the horizon. However, it does not detract from the notion that I am closer to the end than to the beginning.

I am at home under a blue and cloudless sky. It is a feeling that lasts until dawn.

14

In the morning at a newspaper stand near the shrine, I was standing with a group of men looking through the racks of morning papers when the hand touched my shoulder. I looked around and found Jamal smiling excitedly.

'*Shir muse?*' he asked, raising a hand to his mouth and sipping from an invisible glass. I declined his offer but we agreed on getting something to eat. He was anxious to know how things had gone at Hezbollah the day before, but there was no mention of his reluctance to cross the road and follow me in. I didn't push for an answer either, although I had doubtless missed his translation abilities on the day. Secretly I hoped to persuade him to come with me the next time.

At a sidewalk bakery, where men of all ages worked the dough into balls that were then spread onto the inner walls of underfloor ovens, I bought several loaves and we went to a quiet place to eat. It was near to where I had been before with Ahmad, the irate carpet man from the Serai, away from the crush of crowds near the shrine. Pilgrims are usually no problem, but religious infatuation can sometimes be a little hard to digest on a daily basis.

'Did you find your friend?' asked Jamal.

I recounted the events of two days before without much joy and Jamal was sympathetic. He was nineteen and knew nothing of the wars in neighbouring Afghanistan, but still he understood the particular brand of grief I was feeling, the kind that comes from travelling half-way round the world to have your worst fear realised.

'To be honest, Jamal,' I said, 'I could do with your help as a translator. My Farsi still isn't as good as it used to be.'

'Sure,' he replied, but not without a moment's hesitation. There were enough stories floating around most Iranian dinner tables regarding the ferocious nature of Afghans to warrant at least a little caution on his behalf.

We finished one of the loaves and left the other beside a thin man asleep on a bench. The elbows of his jacket were patched and worn and his shoes had seen better days. I noticed a roll of papers sticking out of his trouser pocket and a tidy row of office pens attached to the edge of one of the pages – a reminder perhaps that he had occupied an office chair in the past rather than a seat in a park.

A little way down the street was a contrasting image. Above one of the leading thoroughfares to the holy shrine, an exceedingly obese boy was leaning out of an upstairs window spitting on the black-clothed pilgrims below. The spitting was bad enough, but it just so happened he was naked from the waist up as well. Plump breasts hung over the window-sill as he leaned out to deploy his tiny but well-aimed bomblets of saliva.

The inner courtyard of Hezbollah was busier than the last time. Several little 100-cc Taztac motorbikes, Iranian made, were lined up in the shade of the far wall and their owners were coming down the exterior stairway. I inspected the faces as they passed by but none was familiar.

Upstairs on the landing, Jamal asked a young woman where we could find Baba Khan and in reply, she asked him if he was with the wedding party. He looked amused, as if the thought of going to an Afghan wedding was somehow incredible. Apparently a big wedding was being planned and Hezbollah had something to do with it. Once the confusion was sorted out and Jamal had made it clear that neither of us was either going to a wedding or getting married at one, she led us to where we found Baba Khan at the end of a hall in a white room with a sheet for a door.

15

Hotel Qods, Mashad.

I would like now to tell you what happened in that room. But I cannot. Not because of some secret oath that was sworn, it is simply because there is little of substance that I remember of it. Broad brushstrokes yes, but the detail escapes me. Jamal did most of the talking, while I caught the thread now and then of the conversation. Left to my own devices I would have managed with my gradually improving Farsi, but with Jamal performing the job of translator admirably, I took a back seat. Therefore what happened in that room should be told to you by him. The following is a transcript of his version of the events, recorded later that day on tape.

Is it on?

It's rolling Jamal, so just tell the story you told me earlier.

The whole thing?

Everything you can remember.

OK. Ah, excuse my English.

Your English is very good. You shouldn't worry.

Better than your Farsi at least.

[Laughter] A lot better, now come on, speak.

OK, so, so you got some things wrong the other day. You told me that your friend Nebi was killed in the war.

They told me he had been in a vehicle when it drove over a mine, and that there were many fatalities.

So when we sat down in the room, I am asking Baba Khan to tell us where Nebi is buried. You asked me to ask him this, and Baba Khan looks at me strangely, like I am a little diwaneh – a bit crazy.

I'm sorry.

No, it's all right. It's not your fault. Their Farsi is not good Farsi. Sometimes even I cannot understand their talk. I think it is mixed up with Afghan language a little bit. Would you like some more tea?

Thank you.

[There is a pause while Jamal fills our empty glasses.]

So Baba Khan, he is looking strange and then he asks me what I mean. I tell him I mean Nebi's grave because my friend, that is you, would like to know where he is buried and whether it is possible to go to this place.

That's right. I wanted to pay my respects.

You pay money?

No, it's just an expression in English. I wanted to . . . never mind. Please keep going.

But Baba Khan is shaking his head and saying this is impossible.

Impossible because . . .

Nebi Mohandaspoor, your friend, is alive.

Not dead.

He survived the mine although many others around him were killed.

Not dead.

Praise be to God.

Yes Jamal. Praise be to God indeed.

[The tape ends with the sound of me jumping up and down, punching the air and saying 'Yes!' quite a lot of the time.]

16

This was the best news I had heard in a long time. I was probably in a deeper state of depression than I had realised, and so the rebounding to a state of unbridled joy was felt all the more because of the distance I had to travel to get there. The feeling is impossible to describe completely, except to say that where once there was no hope, there was now its shining opposite. I walked around with a smile on my face for the rest of the afternoon.

The only note of caution to be sounded was that Hezbollah did not know where Nebi had gone to. After the explosion, he had been patched up as best as possible and then taken back to Iran to the hospital in Mashad. That was the end of his role in the war, and seemingly of his contact with Hezbollah as well, although there was no ill-feeling evident in Baba Khan's voice. Nebi was highly respected as one of their greatest fighters, but I could only presume that no one would have blamed him for going his own way. This, however, presented something of a problem. Whilst the news of his survival was gratefully received, there was still a job to do in tracking him down. Jamal had told me that Baba Khan would see to it and that we should return to Hezbollah in a few days, but I knew those few days could turn into weeks, perhaps months, before anything happened. In Afghanistan I had become used to the way in which life was led. It wasn't done to go rushing about all over the place like a mad goose, which meant that Baba Khan would probably get round to finding Nebi later rather than sooner. I needed to start looking on my own. The clock was ticking.

Jamal was now turning into a godsend. His father knew a man at the local government office who dealt with Afghan refugees, and so we agreed to go there early in the morning to make full use of the day.

I slept well that night, more deeply than usual and I wondered whether my body was becoming adjusted to the shape of my single bed, which was higher at the head than at the foot and also inclined slightly towards the wall. The trick was to wedge myself against the wall and use it as a backstop, which also prevented me from sliding down to the foot of the bed in the night.

The next morning I was up at dawn as usual to see the local crane operator ascend dangerously to his place of work and bow before the Imam, his personal insurance agent. Downstairs the other guests were returning from morning prayer, carrying with them the heavenly smell of freshly baked bread. I went off to satisfy my hunger as well and on the way found a small boy selling small clumps of honeycomb dripping with the sweet nectar. It was a breakfast of champions and the mood of optimism that surrounded me was exhilarating.

Unfortunately, this mood was tempered somewhat by the no-show of Jamal. By the time he arrived it was closer to midday than early morning and I had to hide my frustration, reminding myself that he was helping me as a friend. Jamal refused all of my attempts to pay him, but this also meant that I had to abide by his time-keeping. Again, it was like the days of old when I learned to give up my western ideals and adopt the more leisurely approach of the East. But old ways always die hard.

At least we managed to find the refugee office, catching several taxi rides along the wide Mashad roads to our destination. The building was a nondescript affair with a whitewashed wall and iron gate at the front, guarded by a sleepy Iranian soldier. He let us through after sighting my passport and we went up several flights of stairs to a small reception desk, also manned by the military. This man was older, however, and paid greater attention to my passport and its many visa stamps.

He found the ones for Korea and Japan from earlier that year and licked his thumb to turn the pages before finding the stamp for Iran. With a grunt he accepted its authenticity, but then I was slightly unnerved when he placed the passport in a desk drawer and wrote out a receipt for me, saying that I could have it back when I left. There is a rule I almost always follow, and that is to never part with my passport, but on this occasion it seemed I had no choice. He slammed the drawer shut, the impact of which made the keys on his belt jingle against the butt of his revolver.

The room where Jamal's father's friend sat was an airless box filled with filing cabinets. They reached up to the ceiling and covered every wall space except for the window, beneath which was a portly, unshaven man who pulled at the few remaining strands of hair on his head in quiet desperation.

'Where is it?' he kept saying, over and over, until Jamal cleared his throat and interrupted.

The man looked at us as if we had woken him from a bad dream. He half-smiled, but then the crushing weight of reality bore back down and the problem of whatever was lost returned. He started furiously opening and closing the cabinets in a random manner that spoke volumes about his state of mind, which at worst was fast approaching suicidal. We were forced to wait in the corridor for him to calm down.

'Perhaps we should come back tomorrow?' said Jamal.

'No, I'm sure it's all right.'

Not waiting for a reply I barged in and stood in between him and his filing cabinets.

'*Salaam aleikum*,' I said, placing my hand to my heart and offering up a smile. 'I am looking for an Afghan man. His name is Nebi. In the name of God I hope you can help me find him.'

The smile I think did the trick. I could be wrong, but I don't think people smiled a great deal in his office, and especially not at him. The end-of-year party at the Bureau of Immigration, I mused, was not in all likelihood a fun place to be. So a friendly looking face staring at him had an immediate effect. He stopped attacking his metal boxes and regained his composure long enough for Jamal to step in and introduce himself, and then explain our plight.

The man listened. He scratched his head and sighed. I could tell he was thinking this was an easier problem to solve than the one that had vexed him earlier. He moved certainly towards the end of his room and slid open a cabinet that positively bulged with its load of paperwork. Dextrous fingers flicked through to the back and, finding nothing, moved on to the next cabinet. This too groaned with a great weight and with similar adroitness he began searching again. After a few moments, a folder was extracted and opened on his desk.

'Do you know how many Afghan refugees that are in Mashad?' he asked, before replying to his own question. 'Two hundred and fifty thousand.'

I told him I was interested in finding only one and he laughed shrilly.

'*Farghat yek*,' he said. 'Only one.'

I watched his finger work down a line of Persian script to the bottom of a page before it was turned to reveal yet another. He worked his way from the back of the folder to the front, as is the way with all books in Islam which read right to left instead of the opposite.

Finally, however, his finger came down heavily on a single line. We all leaned forward, craning our necks to see, although in my case I was merely looking at an unintelligible scribble.

'Here you are,' said the man excitedly.

'Nebi?' I said, hopefully. But Jamal was not looking so confident.

The portly official continued. 'Soorghul Mushtaaq! You rat! Finally, I have found you.'

Whoever Soorghul was and what he had done wrong I could only guess, but our friend's enthusiasm was not because he had found what we were looking for. Indeed, after another half an hour of waiting while he scoured the pages, Nebi's name refused to appear on the sheets and sheets of paper. There were no Mohandaspoors either. Not a single one.

'Have you tried the Ministry of Internal Affairs in Tehran?' he finally suggested. 'They may be able to help.'

We left him to his task, collected my passport and went out onto the street. The sun was high in the sky and the glare from the building's white-painted walls made it difficult to see.

There was no way I was going back to Tehran. I had previous experience of dealing with the Ministry of Internal Affairs and knew well their endless corridors and mindless minions. There would have to be another way, another place that might have a record of the elusive Nebi Mohandaspoor.

And then it hit me.

'Jamal,' I said. 'Where is the hospital?'

All hospitals keep records of their patients and Baba Khan had clearly said Nebi was taken to one in Mashad after the explosion.

We wasted little time in waving down a taxi headed in the right direction and soon found ourselves within the cool confines of the medical centre.

Neat rows of wheelchairs were parked just inside the main entrance like cabs waiting at a taxi rank. A pair of crutches leaned up against a water-cooler that had water but no cups. Over by the reception desk was a young hospital orderly whom Jamal seemed to recognise. They were shaking hands and smiling at each other, talking it seemed about old times. I didn't intervene, but moments later Jamal waved goodbye to the man and walked over to me. Apparently we were in luck; in fact it was better than luck, it was like hitting the jackpot on a slot machine with your first coin. According to Jamal, this man knew precisely how and where to look for patient records, which had recently been entered into a smart new central computer system. It would be a simple process to check the name of Mohandaspoor and see if anything could be found.

Confirmation that the computer age had reached Mashad could be seen at the reception where a young woman in a black chador was staring with disbelief into a computer screen. She began hitting the same key on the keyboard repeatedly and then stood up with her hands on her hips, glaring down at her off-white coloured nemesis. It blinked back warmly, even kindly, then winked a dot of white light and went black.

Jamal laughed and tisk-tisked.

'Windows 98,' he said disapprovingly.

We waited amidst the ebb and flow of patients and visitors, some carrying flowers and cards, others food. A small boy being led by the hand by his father carried a loaf of flat bread, shaped like an ironing board, that was almost as tall as he was. As the pair walked by, big eyes stared inquisitively at me. I could almost hear his childish thoughts.

'You're not from round here, are you? You're strange. You've got black hair like Dad but there's something about your face. Nose too small? Maybe. And those boots are a dead give-away. What are you doing here?'

Those X-ray eyes were still looking at me from away down the corridor before he tripped over the bread and was scolded for not being careful.

In the end the wait was long, but worth it. The hospital orderly returned and gave Jamal a sheet of computer paper. Incredibly, in black twelve-point type were the details of a young Afghan man named Nebi Mohandaspoor, admitted on 28 August 1989 for extensive leg injuries. He had stayed one month and then left. There was also a phone number.

Jamal pulled out his cellphone and started dialling. It rang a few times and was answered. Jamal spoke and then was quiet as he listened. I was left on the sideline again, watching his nods and his shakes of the head with growing angst. At one stage he glanced at me and made a less than hopeful shrugging motion of his shoulders. Thirteen years was a long time.

Finally, Jamal pushed a button on his phone and slipped it back into his trouser pocket.

'Well?' I said anxiously.

'I am sorry. There is no one there by that name any more. But the woman who answered the phone said she remembered some-one who might have been your friend. He was also Afghan.'

'That's great. Did she say anything else?'

'I think you will not like this, Richard.'

'Try me.'

'She said this person, with his wife and children, returned to the city of Herat in Afghanistan less than a year ago.'

It was the news I had half expected, but dreaded all the same. Now the trail would be doubly hard to follow, although the bad news was tempered slightly with the good. Less than twelve months meant he had gone back to Afghanistan after the fall of the Taliban, which suggested he hadn't become embroiled in that regime or been in harm's way of it. It all made sense; I probably would have done the same thing in his shoes – taken my family away and waited for a time when it would have been safe to return. All things come to pass in Afghanistan, as they do in other parts of the world. But when that time came, like many other Afghans, he would have been helped on his way by the Iranian authorities who were anxious to see as many refugees repatriated as possible. And with the demise of the Taliban, the lure of living in their own country again would have been great.

But there was more, much more. Nebi had a family. He had not only survived, he had made a home. It gladdened my heart to know that things had turned out all right for him.

'So what will you do now?' asked Jamal.

The answer was of course an easy one, but fraught with problems all the same. I would follow Nebi, that much I knew, but I didn't have a visa for Afghanistan (at the time of my departure none were being issued) and there was also the matter of the single-entry visa for Iran stamped into my passport. Having that changed so that I could re-enter Iran to catch my flight home from Tehran wouldn't be easy.

But all along I felt these difficulties were surmountable. I had crossed borders in the past with little in the way of legal documents and even though my daring days of sneaking across frontiers were behind me (two small children who depended on their father to return one day decided that), all the same I knew from these past experiences that border crossings and visas were things that took patience and, at times, a generous donation into the hands of whoever might be inclined to accept such a gift in exchange for turning a blind eye. Initially I would try for legitimacy, then wait to see what other opportunities presented themselves.

'Do you know where the Afghan Embassy is?' I asked finally.

Jamal shrugged in a way that he often used, whenever he didn't know something but was unlikely to admit it. Smart boys from Tehran University weren't normally in possession of such information. Rock groups, movies and sex; these things were known to a certain degree. But the whereabouts of embassies belonging to warring neighbours weren't part of the syllabus. Jamal, however, was developing a surprising determination to help solve my problems and it was proving extremely helpful.

'Come on,' he said, slapping me on the back. 'We'll ask a taxi driver. Although I think there will be trouble if you go to this place.'

'Trouble,' I replied, thinking back to a certain promise I had made to my wife Elisabeth, to try to avoid going to Afghanistan. Wives do not like it when their husbands take off for countries littered with mines; countries that can be relied upon to appear regularly on CNN and not because of a local flower show that had turned up record crowds.

'Oh yes, there will be trouble all right.'

17

Dawn was breaking and I was on a bus. It was a bus with a terminal case of heart disease. On the surface it looked every bit the regular, commuter-issue method of transport circa 1970, possibly press-ganged into service after having done a lifetime's work in Turkey or Germany. Still visible on its faded side panels were the cheerful words REISEN, in heavy type with a coloured outline and slanted over to no doubt impress upon its passengers a sense of speed and urgency. The rest of the paintwork had either been scrubbed out or painted over, or had simply faded in the harsh Afghan sun. Curtains also, which were once a pretty green, now had a lifeless grey tinge to them and were so thin they afforded little shade. There were travel stickers on the back window advertising destinations like Gallipoli and Cappadoccia that harked back to a time before the film *Midnight Express* ruined Turkey's tourist trade. Perhaps that film had also ruined the career of this bus, for it had clearly seen better times and was in the last stages of a death rattle.

This, however, had not dissuaded me from climbing on board and paying the princely sum of two US dollars for the privilege, because there was simply no alternative. It was the day after I had been given the briefest of passes to enter Afghanistan by the Embassy in Mashad, and I was not about to stand around waiting for a better offer.

The Embassy had eventually been found down a back street not far from the city centre, in an alleyway with a few other ambassadorial agencies and residences, each with its own queue of humanity waiting outside. In each case there had usually been a single window with iron bars set into a high wall that stopped anyone from reaching inside and strangling the official who ruled with a casual indifference. Opening hours, and I can speak only for the Afghan Embassy, had been flexible. The window was flung open at periodic intervals just when the crowd had given up hope and wandered off to smoke a cigarette or chat with a disgruntled fellow citizen. Then there would be a headlong rush for the gap in order to fling a passport, application form or money within. Timing had been crucial, but because I didn't smoke and therefore remained stoically at my post, I had managed to get to the front quite early on in the day. Then it had been a matter of appealing to the generosity of the man behind the bars. However, when you are the only one with an actual passport, and this passport has hard currency inside it, it tends to speed things up. My application had been accepted and I was told to report back the next day at 3 p.m. exactly.

Jamal had been a great help in tracking down the Embassy but he could not afford to wait all day outside its walls. He had gone home and I had carried on alone. I was wary of depending on his input too much, not because I didn't need him, far from it, but because I wanted to get back to a degree of self-sufficiency for the times ahead. I had to start speaking Farsi more fluently and to begin judging people by what I could see and hear of them myself, not from what I was told. A translator, even an accidental one like Jamal, distances you from those you meet and numbs the senses that act as an all-important radar.

I had been happy therefore to return the following day to the Embassy and begin what was a lengthy wait inside its walls. Having an application accepted was only part of the story it had seemed, the rest being a drama with comic overtones. After sitting in a small hut built of concrete blocks in the Embassy yard with a host of others for most of the afternoon, marking time by the activities of a trail of ants who were dissecting a larger insect limb by countless limb, I had been instructed to follow a man in a dark suit inside the main building itself. An empty foyer had given way to a similarly uncluttered corridor that led to the office of a man with a vacant expression on his face. This was someone important I realised, by the size of his office and the bored way in which he had attended to his business. On this particular occasion that business had been me, someone without any affiliation to a news team or volunteer agency wanting to enter his country. The conversation had been lively.

'Do you know Allah?' was the first question.

'Not intimately,' was my reply, 'although I believe he is quite nice.'

There had been a shake of the head before the caveat was uttered.

'Because only Allah can protect you. I cannot.'

He had then begun a litany of the things that could happen to me in Afghanistan, being blown up the most likely, death by snake bite and food poisoning coming second equal, while there was a slim chance I might go mad and shoot myself.

I had been prepared to take my chances, since there were some things I had experienced in his country that weren't on his list, ferocious mountain dogs being one of them, but then I wasn't going to tell him I had already been in Afghanistan, illegally for that matter, in far more dangerous times than these. In the end the passport had received a stamp granting permission to enter for ten days. It wasn't much, but it would have to do.

Which brings me back to the bus; the groaning, grizzling beast of burden that presently sat upon the heated tarmac in no-man's-land between Iran and Afghanistan. The driver was underneath, seeing to the undercarriage with a hammer and yelling at the boy who collected the tickets for not being fast enough with the tools. When the driver did emerge he was splattered with oil and wearing a none-too-pleased expression on his grimy face. It didn't help that I was the only passenger either, so profits were clearly as miserable as his mood.

Once we were under way again I was struck by the sheer amount of rubbish that lined the roadside. It seemed the desert was made of torn and tattered plastic bags that clung to bits of wood or barbed wire that lay about the ground. The wind whipped at their edges but the bags held on, fluttering flags of the Republic of Refuse. It wouldn't have taken much to clean up either. Ten men on either side of the road walking abreast of each other would do the job in a few days, but the signs along the way that warned of mines meant no one was game to try. There were no tracks out there, save for the ones that ended abruptly.

This less than scenic path led us straight to the Afghan border post, a typical ramshackle collection of buildings and a tall water tower that doubled as a lookout. Straight away the evidence of refugee camps was obvious, rows of tents behind fences of barbed wire just over the border, although the tens of thousands of refugees reported by the papers to be crossing the border were nowhere in sight. Perhaps they had already been processed and moved on, I couldn't tell. The only sign that anyone was present was the smoke coming from the fire the soldiers had lit to cook breakfast.

We stopped and a grey-green uniformed guard climbed up the steps, AK47 slung over his shoulder. He nodded to the driver and then came to me. My passport was examined and the young shaven face looking down at me smiled. He stuck out his hand. It was cold, but the welcome was a warm one. I followed him outside to a hut where my passport was stamped again and there were more smiling faces as the rest of the soldiers gave up on breakfast and gathered to see the foreigner. Then we were off again, rumbling down the road to the next series of buildings where another guard came on board to check for stowaways, drugs, guns or whatever else was currently on his list of things to look out for. We were waved on and the three of us entered Afghanistan. It was very quick, almost casual, but immediately the air felt different. Behind us lay the security of a reasonably ordered country, where there were things like roads and power lines. Up ahead, there was no road. There were no power lines either, which actually made the landscape seem even more natural. It was suddenly open and vast, as only Afghanistan can be.

Having said that, out of this desert there began to appear more and more houses made from the typical building materials of mud brick and wood. Donkeys appeared carrying huge loads, being driven by small boys with sticks. People sat in the shade of awnings and stood talking beside the road until, with a blast on his horn, the driver had them running towards us.

It was his assistant, the young ticket collector, whose job it was to identify paying customers as we drove along. Most were asking or pleading for a free ride to the next town or village, all of which fell on deaf ears. It was odd to see one so young in such control of the lives of those many years older than himself. He looked about fifteen, but he was dealing with everyone in the same short way. No money, no ride. And when cash was waved in the air, he made damn sure it was enough before a nod to the driver brought the bus to a halt. In this way we inched our way along past the innumerable shantytown houses. Here it seemed was where the refugees had landed, just a few miles inside the border with little in the way of any infrastructure. The houses had simply been built and from these houses people harvested what little they could from the passing traffic. Some had made workshops for engine repairs, others collected scrap metal and piled it metres high on their front doorstep. There was at least water that poured from a smart new manual water pump installed by the UN workers, who sped by us occasionally in dusty white 4WD vehicles heading for Herat. Their journey would be several hours, while ours was beginning to look like it might take days. Once again I had to remind myself of the virtue of patience, especially in a place like this.

When we had at last broken free of this border town I was surrounded by my fellow travellers, grim and dusty and probably resenting the fee they had had to fork out. Some had bundles of wares for sale further down the track, others simply were coming along for the ride. We were a jostling coach of humanity on a journey that would test the nerves of men and the endurance of metal.

The way into Afghanistan is not easy.

In comparison, think childbirth without drugs or a midwife, possibly taking place over a twenty-four-hour period, when out in the open on a sweltering hot day in the middle of nowhere, with a pack of hungry wolves looking on. Or venturing up a jungle creek without the luxury of a canoe, in boots two sizes too small while being shot at by hostile natives who look upon you as a likely candidate for lunch.

Bombed into oblivion over countless years, the road was hardly more than a collection of rough tracks through the desert, pitted with potholes filled with dust that looked solid until you fell into them with a sickening blow to the suspension of your vehicle. Many times throughout the hot day the bus succumbed to this treatment and was forced to limp to the side for repairs, usually tilting at an alarming angle. Then the driver and his boy would get out and crawl underneath the bus to hammer straight whatever was bent, or put back whatever had come unstuck. I'm no mechanic, but I think any such person would have had to admire the way these two managed to get us back on the road again, using only the meagre contents of a toolbox which, when not in use, propped up one side of the driver's seat so that he could sit straight.

The afternoon came and went. Soon the sun was beginning to wilt in the west and the shadows were long across the ground. There was little vegetation, only bare hills on either side, closer on the left than on our right. In that direction I could just make out the trees and bushes that lined the Hari Rud, the river I knew like an old friend. Its wandering course I had followed many times; I had drunk from it, washed in it and taken pleasure from the sight of its crystal-clear waters. Its tributaries had guided me through the mountains on the long walk to Pakistan all those years ago. Now all I could do was stare at it in the distance, hoping that soon we would reach the city through which it ran.

But when for the twentieth time something gave way and we ground to a halt, I began to wonder whether we would ever reach our destination. My fellow travellers were also thinking the same thing. They would heckle the driver which would serve little purpose but to madden him further. Finally, he had had enough and when a few huts appeared on the roadside he swung the wheel hard over and stopped outside the largest one. It turned out to be a sort of restaurant and watering hole, but one look inside told me there would be no Michelin-rating here. From a barrel I accepted the stale bread on offer and used it to bat away the flies that swarmed to my plate of meat and rice. The sugary tea, however, had a positive effect and I felt some strength return. I had been gripping the seat in front of me now for so many hours my forearms hurt like hell and my back was aching. Worse still, my head was throbbing with pain from dehydration. Stupidly I hadn't taken enough water with me and I was beginning to have trouble seeing clearly. Once we were back in the bus, all I could do was continue to hold on with my eyes partially closed. In this way I watched darkness fall, the light of our headlights showing the way forward.

When at last we came to Herat it was late at night. No one had the strength to say anything, let alone cheer. The driver took us through the outskirts and came to the city centre where most of us disembarked with our belongings. I stood there as the others melted away into the darkness, each with his or her own mission to accomplish or home to find, and watched the twin tail-lights of the bus move off.

It suddenly occurred to me I had nowhere to stay, nor any knowledge of such a place. The last time I was in Herat, it was on the outskirts where the mujahedeen held sway. With my Hezbollah friends, Nebi included, we slept in the cellars of bombed-out houses where there was better protection against a stray mortar or other such missiles. We never came to the city centre which was occupied by the enemy, the Soviet-backed government forces. From our own secure places we could hear the city, its traffic and people, but we could never see them. Now I was on the side of a busy road where the lights of passing trucks and vehicles were almost the only illumination. It was practically pitch-black. There were buildings, the largest of which was across the road, but not a single lamp shone from its windows. Behind me was a row of low shops that had a glowing light bulb above each door, powered by a small generator that putt-putted from somewhere in the dark. But these lights were meagre and a few men gathered beneath them like moths. One such group I walked up to and asked for help in finding a hotel. They eyed me suspiciously. One man lifted up an arm and pointed at the building across the road.

'*Unjah?*' I said.

'*Unjah,*' came the reply.

Apparently I was peering through the darkness at the only hotel in Herat, when as if by magic, a sudden burst of light cast back the shadows. I dropped my bag and stood gawping at a wondrous sight, an oasis in the desert. It had surely seen better days, but right at that moment, with every part of my body crying out for a bed or even a piece of floor to lie on, there was nothing so glorious as the Hotel Mowafaq.

18

M y notebook reads:

I wake at 2 a.m. It is quiet now. Only the dogs rouse the night as they bark at each other across the city. There is a sudden yelping which brings a halt to their canine conversation. They listen. I listen. The city pauses mid-breath, mid-stride, waiting to know – when a single bark is heard in the distance.

'It's all right,' it seems to be saying. 'I just stubbed my paw.'

The others return with howls of derision, 'You stupid mutt!'

I lie back and close my eyes, when there comes another sound which the dogs also seem to take heed of. It is a heavy, slow, rhythmic tapping of wood on stone; two distinct sounds, tip-tap, tip-tap, tip-tap, like a man on stilts. Then it is gone. Swallowed whole by the night. As if it had never existed. What was that sound? Am I dreaming again?

At dawn my first impression was that this was a hard-looking city. The word 'brutal' was not quite right, but only just did it miss the mark. It was hot and dusty, filthy and fly-ridden, and the gutters were filled with a stench unimaginable.

The hotel was four floors high near a major intersection and my room looked out over all of it. I had a grandstand view of hell. Acres and acres of flat-topped houses crowded in amongst each other with high walls of mud brick surrounding court-yards in which little bare-bottom children wandered.

Or at least it was hell in comparison to the Herat I had imagined. The open spaces and quiet streets of my Herat were gone, replaced by a typically ugly urban sprawl. From my old mujahedeen homes in the outlying areas, I had pictured Herat as an extension of my own surroundings which even though they were bombed and broken, at least had fields of untended fruit trees watered by small irrigation streams. Even the rows of pine trees I had once viewed from afar and saw as a thing of beauty, on closer inspection were dull and dusty.

Ironically, right beside the hotel was the old water tower which the fighters of Hezbollah used as a rangefinder for their artillery. Not far away also was the old citadel that had been the object of both fear and hatred amongst the men. An ancient place, built on an outcrop of rock by Alexander the Great centuries ago, it still looked impregnable. I had been told it was there any captured mujahedeen were taken for interrogation and then death. It was said their bodies were then thrown from the battlements to tumble down and be consumed by the dogs below, although I wondered even then whether this was a way to get the men to fight harder.

Now, looking from my hotel room at its three vast rounded towers and many smaller square-shaped turrets, I could begin to believe the warning. Unlike old buildings in other countries that are more of the picture-postcard variety, whose possible evil history has long since faded in the camera flash of tourism, the fort overlooking Herat retained its ambience of menace.

But from my eyrie I had to ask, where was Nebi in all of this?

Down on the street I found a place to eat a breakfast of bread and tea. Every table was infested with flies and I had to jealously guard my meal from their invasion. They were everywhere – on the floor, the walls, the ceiling and the owner, a dirty man in his later years who had given up all hope of fending them off. Sitting at his desk with an old cash register before him, he played host to the millions; a mother to an insect world.

Outside, children aged between one and ten years old played in the dirt. One of the youngest had a tin of pineapple but no visible means to open it. So she sucked on the rim and kept looking at the label, perplexed as to why pineapples didn't taste as good as they looked.

All the while cars, trucks, motorbikes, bicycles and buses, horses and carts flowed past in the street. The larger vehicles all had the same special whooping whistle the drivers used often to scatter anyone foolish enough to stand in their way. There was even a 4WD vehicle from one of the international rescue missions which had broken down and was being helped along by a crowd of children, all pushing from the rear. Just who was saving who?

I ate as quickly as I could and left the remainder to the flies, conscious that I had to make use of every day if I was to have any chance of finding Nebi. I decided to accept an offer I had received upon checking into the hotel. Hamid was an Afghan 'Jamal', an English-speaking twenty-year-old who was wise beyond his years and worked behind the front desk. Hamid had profited from the sudden influx of journalists from all the leading papers and television channels once the Taliban had been ousted. The world media paid a hundred US dollars per day for his translation services. They paid almost the same to be driven around by his older friend, Abdul Latiff. I, on the other hand, did not have their expense accounts and it took quite some time to convince Hamid of this, but in the end we came to a commercial arrangement. I paid for lunch and bought the petrol.

That first day was a journey back in time. I asked Abdul Latiff to drive us to the village of Jibrail where I had spent much time with Hezbollah. It lay to the west of the city, where most of the fighting raged in those long years of war against the Russian invaders. Perhaps there might be some clue there as to the whereabouts of Nebi? It wasn't much to go on but it was a start.

Within minutes the ugly central part of the city was behind us. The transformation from hell to something a little more picturesque was dramatic. Gone was the smell of the open sewer and the flies too were no longer a plague. Abdul took us directly past the old minarets that have stood for centuries as a reminder of the vision of Herat's first glorious architects. Though fewer in number than when I had last viewed them, they were still hugely impressive. To stand in their shadow and see them up close was far more than I could have dreamed of the last time, their location being in a part of Herat that lay between the two sides, a sort of unofficial no-man's-land. Back then I had tried to get close and nearly died in the attempt. It was Nebi who pulled me clear of the sniper's bullet, and it wasn't the only occasion when his timely intervention had saved my skin.

Further on past the minarets it was as if I was back in 1989. Nothing seemed to have changed. The bombed-out villages were still there; the trails that weaved their way in and out and over old destroyed buildings remained in use. Only the odd shiny metal water pump was evidence of any progress. It was suddenly quiet and calm, a rural setting with streams that burbled their way past overhanging mulberry branches beneath a wide blue sky. I was overjoyed to be back, and amazed as well.

In a short space of time I had located the old Hezbollah *komiteh* or base. It was just off a broad avenue lined with clumps of pine trees which made for easily recognisable landmarks. In one direction the road travelled back towards the border with Iran, back towards the villages of Sangbast and Shekiban. I had walked along its path many times and for many miles, but never had I known its opposite end which led into Herat. It was fascinating to see how close our *komiteh* was to the city centre all that time. By foot, it was no more than a twenty-minute stroll. And the sections of earth that I knew to be mined were now being dug up to install floodwater pipes to prevent the city becoming a lake in the seasonal downpours of rain. There also in the near distance was the water tower beside the Hotel Mowafaq, rising up amongst the pine trees. It all started to form a greater picture. Whereas before I had only a limited idea of my surroundings, now I was able to see how this piece of the puzzle joined up with this other piece. It was incredibly overpowering and to Hamid and Abdul Latiff I must have been an amusing sight, bursting with wonder at retracing old steps, running into houses of rubble and saying, 'Here, here! It was here we sat and cooked our meals. Over in this room was the wash-house. And this is where we would sleep, our waist-coats folded into pillows!'

In a neighbouring field I could even see the pile of stones that marked the grave of the stranger who had walked into our camp, shot in the chest and in desperate need of blood. He died in the cellar with a look of complete resignation on his face, having given up on the struggle to live. I remember thinking how it could have been me, an anonymous grave in a place no one in my family would know about, visited only by the passing herds of indifferent goats.

Sadly, the ruins of the *komiteh* were just that, nothing but empty ruins. Along the avenue which had been coated in a thin layer of metal stones there were a few stores that had opened for business. Passing one of these on foot, we had been ushered in by a venerable old man with a Father Christmas beard and smile. A small boy was despatched to bring tea and we were seated in the shade of the awning outside his shop. I noticed the ditch on the side of the road by our feet was now flowing fully with clear water. Someone somewhere had chosen to redirect the stream, which also served to drop the air temperature around us by one or two degrees. Abdul Latiff sat on his haunches and washed his hands and feet before ambling off to pray.

The elderly man was naturally curious to see us, especially me. While Hamid explained what little he knew of the reasons for me coming to Herat, the old man nodded and smiled and kept looking at me with eyes that twinkled bright blue. When he spoke it was with a hoarse voice that strained to get above much more than a whisper. I noticed a long scar running down his neck from behind his ear. It eventually disappeared behind his turban that was draped over one shoulder and fell into his lap.

'The old man tells me he has been in this part of Herat all his life,' said Hamid.

I was surprised.

'Even during the war?' I asked.

The old man nodded and held up two fingers. 'Both wars,' he said, referring not only to the war against the Russians but also to the most recent conflict against the Taliban.

'America *khoob*!' he exclaimed happily, and with his hands he mimicked the flight of an aeroplane that zoomed over our heads and dropped a single bomb. Then from a clasped position his hands parted rapidly and he held them out wide in the perfect description of a powerful explosion.

'The Americans dropped a bomb on the Taliban head-quarters and the next day they were gone,' said Hamid with a smile. 'Everyone was happy. Everyone loves the Americans for doing this.'

It turned out the Taliban occupied an old Hezbollah building that I knew well. I had spent a few days there during my first week in Herat. It was Hezbollah's main fort and well defended if memory served me right. At least it had weathered the Soviet bombardment through the years, but later in the day we would drive by the ruins and witness what the modern age of powerful, laser-guided missiles could do to mud brick and stone.

Eventually tea arrived at the old man's store, followed by a different kind of bombshell. In the course of our talk the name of Haji Qarry Ahmad Ali was mentioned. Immediately I asked Hamid to explain how I knew this Hezbollah commander personally and the old man sat up straight in his chair.

'Old one arm!' he said, chopping a hand against his elbow. 'Haji Qarry is a very good man. He fought near here during the first war.'

I told him then that I was with Haji Qarry during this time, living for a while in a *komiteh* just a stone's throw away. It was one of Haji Qarry's men that I now sought.

The old man stroked his beard and began to eye me closely. Then he leaned forward and tapped me on the knee.

'Now I remember,' he said quietly.

Hamid did the rest of the translation job that day because the old man suddenly spoke so quickly and excitedly I couldn't keep pace. Little things I managed to understand, but the majority was out of reach of my Farsi. And so Hamid fed me the information bit by bit as it came along. He himself was amazed that the old man sitting down with us could remember the foreigner who arrived in western Herat with Hezbollah.

'BBC, yes?' said the old man, a finger pointed at my chest before he broke out once more into a verbal sprint. It wasn't quite true however. The description of me as a BBC journalist was something Hezbollah had proffered and I had not refuted, simply because it was a convenient label. I'm sure they themselves preferred to believe in it, what with the resulting kudos someone like this in their company would bring. Now it seemed this was a correct assumption.

He remembered an enormous amount, some things even I had forgotten of that time. Like the old tank turret that sat out on the road. I had a photograph at home of a group of men sitting on it proudly like hunters in the evening light, as if they were the ones who had just made the kill. The turret was gone now, taken away by the Taliban for spare parts.

He also recalled the bullet-ridden yellow Mercedes taxi that we used for target practice. It too had been dragged away several years ago and was more than likely put back into service.

There was, however, one more thing I hoped the old man would remember.

'Do you know Nebi Mohandaspoor?' I asked.

'Yes, yes,' came the immediate reply, then he started speaking quickly again to Hamid who listened intently. It seemed a long time before Hamid turned to me and spoke.

'Nebi was injured and taken to Mashad,' said Hamid.

'I know.'

'Then he returned to Herat after the Taliban fled.'

'I know this also.'

'And now he works in a shop near the hotel.'

'You're joking!'

It couldn't be that easy I thought. Just walk into Afghanistan looking for someone you haven't seen in thirteen years and the third person you meet knows where he works? Surely not.

19

Of course nothing is ever that easy in Afghanistan. It is a country that simply does not work with such well-oiled precision. Fairytales happen elsewhere.

The place we drove to was a carpenter's workshop where Nebi had worked occasionally in the first few months after having returned to Herat. But that was over a year ago and now the only clue was a report he had gone to the village of Pashtun Zargon, about twenty or thirty kilometres to the east. I checked with Hamid and yes, Abdul Latiff could take us there, but not today. Today he had to pick up the children from school and buy some food at the market for his family. Besides, it was a long journey that would take most of the day.

'But I could walk that distance in a day,' I said with a wry grin.

'The roads are very bad,' he replied gravely, not noticing my smile, and so I left it at that. I was anxious not to upset the two people who had already given me such help – and such hope.

For the rest of the day I walked and eventually stumbled across the central hospital which displayed a sign bearing a picture of a Kalashnikov rifle with a cross through it. The hospital was on one of the wide avenues that are part concrete slab and part pothole, radiating out from the main intersection outside my hotel. Some of these wide roads had a distinctly Russian feel to them, like the ones found leading to and from the airport in Moscow, although not quite as large or as long.

Nevertheless, they were in a sad state and were devoid of any lane markings. Then again, so were the roads in Moscow.

Another reminder of that tragic relationship Afghanistan had with the Kremlin was hobbling out of the main gates on crutches as I was passing. She was a small girl about ten years old with a prosthetic leg that looked to be a few inches too long for her, so she was forced to swing the prosthetic limb out sideways to stop it hitting the ground at every step. It was a terribly pathetic scene, more so because she was all dressed up in a pretty coloured frock that sparkled with bits of glitter around the hem. Too young for the *burqa,* her parents had probably bought the dress so that she could wear it for her homecoming. They walked beside her now, a mother all in blue from head to toe and an anxious father who struggled to raise a smile at his daughter's recovery. The false leg had probably ruined her chances of a normal life with a husband and children, and although the little girl did not know it, he did. For the moment, however, she was the happiest little thing, beaming in her decorative party dress and racing to get home as fast as she could.

As any father would with a young daughter, I felt the pain that was all too obvious on his face.

Further on was the Iranian Embassy, clearly visible from the red, white and green flag that hung from a pole above the guardhouse. The wall was so high it was difficult to see over, but when a car drove in through the iron gates I caught a glimpse of gardens of roses within.

Standing next to a small window in the wall were two men waiting in line. Metal crash barriers were erected to prevent chaos and to create orderly queues, but today it seemed there were few who wanted a ticket to Iran. In Herat you could drink alcohol, you were not ruled by mullahs and had greater freedom of speech since the Taliban ruled no longer. Emigration over the border, except to do business, was obviously not high on anyone's wish list.

That being said, it was for me. Not to emigrate but to ensure that I would be able to get back into that country to catch my flight out when the time came. I had already had visions of having to journey to Kabul and from there fly to somewhere

The ancient citadel of Pai Hesar, Herat

Outside the Hotel Mowafaq, Herat

Seoshan village, near He

Local transport, Herat city

Herat's 800-year-old Friday Mosque

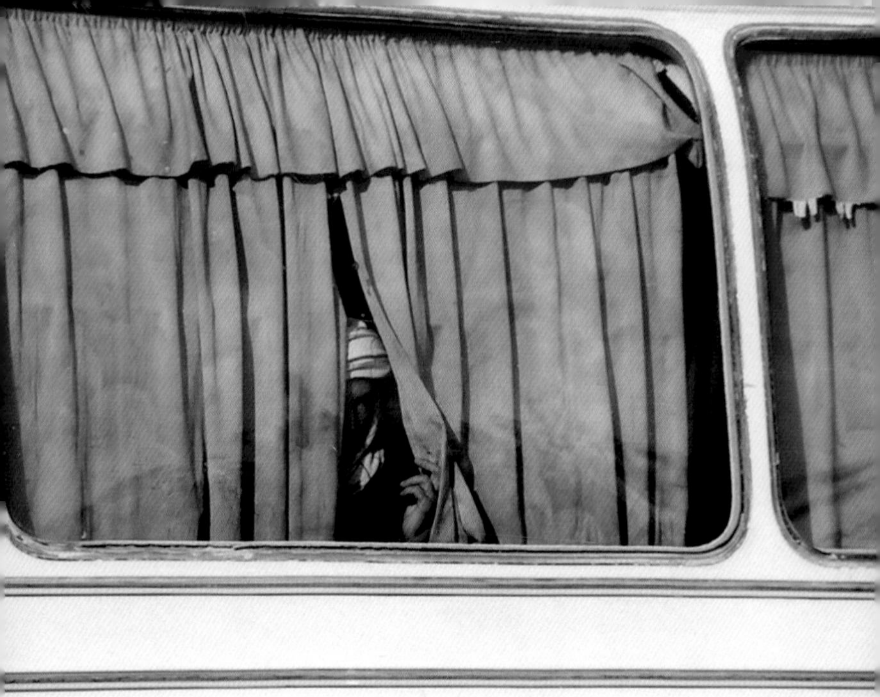

At the Afghan bor

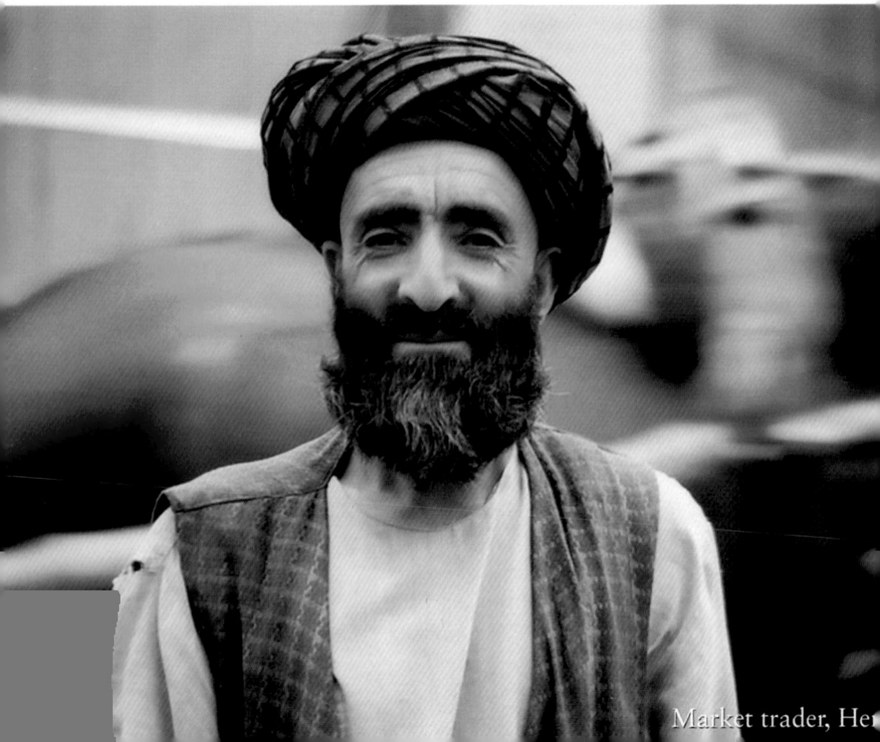

Market trader, He

Village life

The 'Inventor of Herat'

A young mine victim

Pashtun Zorgan

In the mountains

Seoshan, Herat province

Store owner, Herat

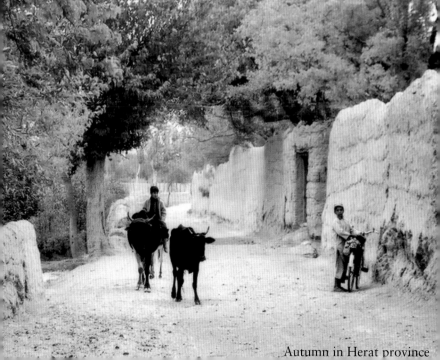

Autumn in Herat province

Jibrail village, western H

Green fields of H

like Islamabad in Pakistan. But the sight of the Embassy reminded me I now needed a new visa back into Iran.

Fortunately, it was a simple enough task, although there were a few questions as to why I hadn't been given a multiple-entry visa in the first place, one that would allow me to go in and out of Iran on several occasions. I told them this was easier said than done and that the Embassy in London had been allowed only to give out single-entry visas to travellers. At this they threw up their hands and shook their heads with dismay. I was glad to see that the Iranian government policies were as strange to their employees as they were to me.

However, there was one catch. The only visa they could offer me now was a transit visa. Seven days only from the time I entered the country, which in theory would be long enough to get to Tehran, but not to do much else. I still hadn't spent as much time with Hezbollah in Mashad as I had planned, catching up with anyone else I might know there. Alas, no amount of pleading would change the minds of the men behind the window. What was done was done, and I would have to return to the Embassy in a few days to collect my passport.

On the way back to the hotel, a lorry-load of prosthetic limbs drove into the hospital and started to unload. Many were of adult size, but only a few looked as though they might suit the body of a child.

My room at the Mowafaq (imagine a concrete floor covered in a thin rug, two single beds, one of which I jammed against the door that opened onto a rusty balcony because there was no lock, and a toilet that spewed water across the floor whenever it was flushed) was on the top floor at the far end of a long hall. As such, it was the last room to receive anything like power and water, which had the habit of turning from a trickle to a torrent at the most unexpected time. Likewise, if someone up the hall turned on a light, then my own solitary bare bulb would dim.

The hotel worked off a generator, as did everything else in Herat, and so you could never be sure what you were going to get from one minute to the next. It was why the building had been in darkness the previous night when I had climbed down from the bus. The generator had done whatever generators do when they've had enough of life, and it had agreed to work again only when coerced into doing so by Hamid.

According to the papers the local governor, Ismail Khan, a noted military commander of the Jamiat-i-Islami mujahedeen during my time in Herat, had recently done a deal with Turkmenistan to provide electricity for the city, but so far it was a promise he had yet to fulfil.

The good news was that change was happening for the people of Herat. Someone had started painting the concrete seats in a small park nearby a baby-pink colour with sky-blue edging. Maybe this was the deal with the Uzbeks – power for paint. There was a fountain that had been draped in a tarpaulin, and underneath it looked suspiciously like a group of leaping dolphins that might one day spout water playfully from their mouths: an altogether strange sight in a city so far from the sea.

There were also rows and rows of rose bushes covered in the dust that billowed up from the roads. Almost all of them were red, backing up the story I'd read somewhere of Herat in the old days before the most recent wars, when men strolled the streets with roses clasped regally behind their backs. Then, Herat was called the City of Gardens, but there was still hope that it would one day live up to that heritage.

Hamid voiced this when he said Herat would soon be the new Paris, although he wasn't entirely sure what Paris looked like. True, there were some comparisons to be made. The towering minarets were not unlike the Eiffel Tower, the Hari Rud could be the Seine, and the old fort might just pass for La Bastille on a hazy summer's day with your eyes half closed.

That night I found him downstairs in the reception, watching television. The programme was a black-and-white puppet show with two characters beating each other up with clubs: an Afghan Punch and Judy show. Seated in comfortable armchairs on either side of him were heavily bearded men with long, flowing turbans. None took their eye off the show when I greeted them. Their mouths muttered salutary replies and their right hands moved to their hearts in the Muslim tradition, but this was clearly prime-time TV and nothing was going to disturb them while it was on. I took a plastic chair from a pile in the corner and went out to sit on the front doorstep.

There was another man there also, smoking in the semi-darkness. With every puff I could see the glow from his cigarette briefly flare up and then fade, which made me feel as though I was playing a bit part in a detective movie. Any minute now there would be the spit of a silenced pistol and the thud of body hitting floor, then footsteps running from the scene of the crime, leaving behind the beautiful girl crouching low over her dead lover and . . .

'*Salaam aleikum*,' he said.

I woke up, staring into a kindly face framed by a dark brown *cola*, the typical Afghan hat worn by men from the Panshir Valley, north of Kabul. He flicked the rest of his cigarette to the gutter and held out his hand. I grasped it firmly.

'*Aleikum salaam*,' I replied.

He winced with pain.

'What is it with you westerners? You must crush a man's hand in greeting him.'

I noticed his hand was tightly bandaged.

'Sorry. I didn't mean to . . . It's just something my father taught me.'

'Don't worry,' he said with a smile, shrugging away the incident. 'My father also was a teacher. I am Ghollum Sefarr, by the way.'

There was something about Ghollum Sefarr that was different from most other Afghans. Perhaps it was a well-fed look. Although not fat by any means, in fact far from it, he lacked the slightly haggard appearance of the average man in the street. Even his teeth gleamed white and were all accounted for as far as I could tell, which added to the healthy glow that seemed to surround him. His clothes were neat, his beard trimmed and I noticed the fingernails in his unbandaged hand were straight and even. He was beginning to make me feel unkempt.

The reason for Ghollum Sefarr's condition soon revealed itself when he said he worked for the Italian Embassy in Kabul. It was one of the best jobs going, given that the Italians looked after their people probably more than any other diplomatic service.

The Americans brought Coke and burgers, the British port and brandy, while the Italians imported their entire country.

He was in Herat to oversee the safe transit of a convoy of trucks coming in from Iran. Getting over the border was hard enough, he said, but the real fun and games started once inside Afghanistan. There was money to be paid to local authorities in Herat, money to be paid to the soldiers who patrolled the entry and exit points around the city, and then there was the task of running the gauntlet to Kandahar and from there up to Kabul. Kandahar province particularly worried him because of the armed gangs that roamed the hills with nothing better to do, now that they were no longer in the employ of the Taliban, than to extract an informal road tax from passing trucks such as his. Sometimes they also took the trucks and their contents, so now he had organised hired guns to ensure a safe passage. The pasta would, it seemed, get through this time.

But there was much more to Ghollum Sefarr than just his job. We were about the same age and so had lived through similar times. When I was a boy hearing about the Russian invasion of his land and taking an interest in it, he was watching the soldiers ransack his home and then set it on fire. They took his brothers away and tried to conscript them into the army, but both escaped and joined the ranks of mujahedeen under the leadership of the legendary Ahmad Shah Massoud. It was a common ploy by the invaders to try and get Afghans to fight Afghans, and it had worked to some degree – young boys taken away to training camps and taught to fight their own with the help of brainwashing techniques and mass hypnosis. Then after the war when the Russians had retreated, there was the problem of what to do with these recruits. Slowly they started drifting back to the towns and villages they had been taken from. Many did not know their families any more or what they looked like. At the airports, he said, anxious parents waited, holding up cards with a name on it, hoping that person would recognise it as their own.

Ghollum Sefarr had fought as well, defending the Panshir Valley with his father's old British rifle in the early years, before modern equipment like Stinger anti-aircraft missiles and AK47s became available.

'What happened to the rifle?' I asked.

'Under the bed.'

'And it still works?'

'Of course. If you come and visit me in the Panshir, we will go hunting with this rifle. You must come in the spring. Not now, soon it will be very cold and the way in will be closed.'

I accepted his invitation graciously. The thought of returning after the winter to the parts of Afghanistan I had never seen was a compelling idea, but with a grin I told him my wife might not agree as readily to the idea. He laughed and showed off his pearly white teeth.

'Is she Italian?'

'No, she's English.'

'Ah, then you will be all right. The English women are nice and gentle, but the Italian women are to be feared.'

Just then a phone started ringing nearby. Not an old-fashioned ring, but a modern cellular call. Immediately Ghollum Sefarr reached into his waistcoat and pulled out a satellite phone. His conversation was in Dari, the native Afghan language that is very similar to Farsi, but I could tell by his body language that he was talking to his employers. Finally, he turned off the phone and slipped it halfway back into his pocket before withdrawing it once again.

'Would you like to call her?' he asked.

'Who?'

'Your woman.'

Not being too up with the play regarding satellite phones I was a little taken aback.

'You mean I can just dial home from here?'

'Sure,' he said.

'But it will be expensive, won't it?'

'One US dollar per minute. That is all.'

I thought for a moment as to what I might say. 'Hi it's me! I'm in Afghanistan and all is well. It's a clear night and I can see the stars. How are the children?'

It seemed absurdly simple, even slightly wrong. The day's events, being in Herat again, everything had transported me back to a time when phones still had cords attached and computers were only just becoming available. The Internet was a dream and telex machines ruled the earth as the only means of global communication. To be handed a six-inch-long piece of plastic with a stubby aerial and be given the chance to call home didn't seem right. I wasn't prepared. In the end, I used the different time zone as an excuse. It would be roughly four in the morning at home, but later I would rue the missed opportunity.

20

The Toyota sedan belonging to Abdul Latiff bumped and lurched along a double rut of dust, rocks and stones banging against the underside of the chassis. Hamid sat in the front while I held on in the back. We crossed a shallow riverbed and almost became stuck. A flock of fat-tailed sheep watched us from the opposite riverbank and then trotted off as we came near.

Up ahead the country was slowly turning a beautiful autumn amber. Clumps of beech trees that gathered along the streams were resplendent in their coats of gold against a bright blue sky. Here and there, villagers were bent over in fields of bright green with their hands in the soil. Some would look up as we passed, most likely because Abdul had the stereo turned up high and one of Afghanistan's most famous singers was blasting out another love song.

Hamid started beating out the rhythm with his feet on the floor and yelling like a tuneless lunatic. He was hopelessly out of synch.

'*Ahgrab*! *Ahgrab*!' he yelled.

Then I remembered *ahgrab* meant scorpion and the offending creature was running around inside Abdul Latiff's vehicle. I swung my feet up onto the seat as we came to a sudden halt, sending clouds of dust into the car and making it nearly impossible to see anything, let alone a poisonous animal.

Hamid thumped again with his feet, and again. Then he and

Abdul Latiff jumped out and stood on the road.

'Did you get it?' I said.

'No.'

I opened my door and climbed out, noticing that the other two men wore open-toed sandals as opposed to my own walking boots. I had to laugh, because Hamid especially was probably not used to going much further afield than his front desk at the hotel.

'These aren't good shoes for Afghanistan,' I said, pointing at his exposed toes.

He mumbled something but I couldn't tell what. His main concern was where the scorpion had gone. No one was getting back into the car until the wee nasty was located, and despite our subsequent searching it remained as elusive as Nebi.

I looked over the roof of the car at the mountains which reared up before me, only a day's walk away. The gateway to an interior I knew well, but one which I had not the time to explore again. The village of Pashtun Zargon was our destination this day, and according to Abdul Latiff it was just a few miles further on. I suggested we walk.

'Walk?' Hamid exclaimed. 'We have a car, why do you want to walk?'

'You mean we have a car with a deadly scorpion lurking somewhere inside it.'

He agreed that the scorpion had changed things and possibly it wasn't too clever to go on without first finding it. However, it was also getting late in the day and the darkness came quickly in Afghanistan at this time of year. It might take hours.

It was mutually decided that we would leave the car on the side of the road and continue on foot to the village. Abdul Latiff knew the headman who would put us up for the night. He also knew the car would be safe in these parts.

'No one can drive,' he said.

We started off in silence and soon I was far enough ahead to begin to enjoy the feeling of walking alone again. This was my element, my country and there was nothing ahead that would be strange or foreign. The city felt alien, but here in the open I was becoming more and more at home with each step. Walking also helps me to think and plan, and I chose this time to make a few careful decisions.

Finding Nebi was paramount to the success of my journey. Though some people might have felt happy at coming so far, I knew I would kick myself later for not exhausting every possibility. Pashtun Zargon was one such stone that had to be looked under, which in turn might well lead somewhere else. I would continue until the leads ran out, or all hope was gone, regardless of the limitations of my visa. Overstaying would mean being forced to leave the country, and since that was what I intended to happen eventually, it would probably be worth the risk.

Hezbollah were also a sort of trump card. Baba Khan in Mashad may have some information by now which would help, and I would have to call him on my return to Herat.

About an hour later, Hamid caught up to me as we closed in on the city.

'Abdul Latiff says the village chief will be able to help you find your friend. He knows everyone.'

'That is good.'

'He also says not to mention the Taliban.'

'Why is that?'

'Because,' he said, pausing to find the right words, 'it might cause trouble. For some villages the Taliban have gone. But for others it is a problem.'

It was a gentle reminder that Afghanistan's past was never far from its present. The two revolved around each other in a merry dance. Perhaps Pashtun Zargon had a few hidden secrets that were best not brought to the surface.

'I'll mind my P's and Q's,' I promised.

Hamid nodded and then his face lit up.

'P's and Q's. I know this expression. It is in my English book at school.'

'You're still at school?' I asked.

'Advanced English,' he replied. 'The classrooms are next to the hotel. You should come and sit in on one of the lectures.'

'Thank you,' I said. 'I will.'

A short while later Abdul Latiff led us through a narrow series of lanes that were made concave by the centuries of traffic, both man and animal. On either side smooth walls of baked earth rose up perhaps twelve feet high. Their main construction was of sun-dried mud bricks which were then coated in a cement-like substance made of straw, animal waste and earth mixed with water. This was how they lasted so long and were so easy to repair. The basic ingredients for a good, strong wall were everywhere.

At regular intervals wooden doors appeared in the walls and it was on one of these that Abdul Latiff banged his fist. After a few moments of scurrying and the sound of women's voices, an elderly man opened the door and clapped his hands when he saw Abdul Latiff. They kissed on each cheek and it took them both several minutes to get through the pleasantries of asking after family members and the health of one's cow. He greeted us with similar accord, albeit a toned-down version, and we were ushered through into a small courtyard with steps leading up to the living quarters on the second floor. Downstairs I caught sight of a young girl milking a cow.

Haji Sardegh was the village chief. In actual fact there were two chiefs but apparently Haji Sardegh was senior in terms of his position as well as his years. His physical stature, however, was tiny. Abdul Latiff had to bend a long way down to greet him and Abdul Latiff was not an overly tall man either.

That being said, Haji Sardegh made up for his physical presence with an air of nobility that wrapped itself around him like a cloak. With his grey beard and brilliant white *shalwar camise* and turban, he demanded respect and was given it. Once we were seated on the floor and tea was laid at our feet, Abdul Latiff honoured him with a few words to Hamid and myself regarding Haji Sardegh's accomplishments over the years. He had fought the Russians and captured a tank single-handedly. He had shot at the helicopter gunships with nothing more than a pistol and devised devious traps to capture the enemy.

But of the Taliban, as expected, nothing was mentioned.

The praise must have worked for it wasn't long before a meal of rice and vegetables better than anything I had seen or tasted so far was carried in. There were tomatoes and aubergine cooked in oil and fresh bread to use as a spoon. The rice was delicious and it was some time before I remembered the reason for being in Pashtun Zargon in the first place.

I asked Hamid to enquire if Haji Sardegh knew anything of Nebi Mohandaspoor.

The old man looked up to the ceiling and pondered. He took off his turban and ran a hand over his bald head before replacing it in a thoughtful kind of way. It is always polite in Afghan circles to say why you are looking for someone, in case that someone does not want to be found. So I piped up and in my best Farsi explained that Nebi was a friend I had not seen in many years. Haji Sardegh listened and nodded before ignoring me completely and speaking directly to Abdul Latiff, who then spoke to Hamid who then spoke to me. It seemed there was a pecking order and I was bottom of the food chain.

'Haji Sardegh,' said Hamid, 'would like to know where you learned to speak Farsi.'

'In Afghanistan,' I replied to Haji Sardegh.

More words were spoken along the line of command until they were again delivered to me by Hamid.

'Haji Sardegh also asks if you believe in the one true God.'

There is one thing I have learned in my time spent travelling through Islam and that is the Kalimeh, a line from the *Koran* which I had long since committed to memory, precisely for moments like these.

'*Bismillah-hir rahmani rahim la illa heh il-la lah Mohammadu rasulu-lah.*'

It means: 'In the name of God, the most benevolent and merciful, there is one true God and Mohammad is his messenger.'

Haji Sardegh actually nodded in my direction this time, but still spoke to Abdul Latiff. This time it was for a lot longer and I sensed I was getting somewhere. Eventually I discovered through Hamid what I came to find. The stone was turned over and examined, but there was no Nebi in Pashtun Zargon.

21

I don't know why I dream dreams. Sometimes they are nothing more than a collection of half-remembered events from the distant past regurgitated into a haphazard story without beginning or end.

But sometimes they amount to something more.

The trick, of course, is to recognise the difference between the two. Which isn't difficult if in one dream you are being chased by a marshmallow the size of New York, and in the other you are being spoken to by someone who seems to know what you are on about, prompting you to do nothing but sit there and listen, without the need of a voice.

The latter, in my case, tends to pose more questions than answers. At least that is how it seems. But the thing is, they are often the right questions. The ones that really matter.

And so, in the middle of an Afghan night, I wake up on the floor of Haji Sardegh's house, not knowing which way is up or down because it is pitch-black, with the following words in my head.

'What have you forgotten?'

That is all. 'What have you forgotten?' burning a hole in my brain and ringing soundlessly in my ears. It nags at me, it teases me. I sit up and try to make my eyes work in the dark, so that I might better see and understand. Slowly they adjust and I scan the room for signs of my sleeping companions. Two shapes over to the right: Abdul Latiff and Hamid.

Then for some reason a photograph comes to mind, the only one I ever took of Nebi. He is sitting in front of the old Russian troop carrier captured by Hezbollah during the war and smiling into the camera. It takes me back to the days when he would spend hours keeping that truck going. No one else seemed to know how it worked. The instructions that appeared on many of its parts were written in Russian, but Nebi knew. Nebi knew engines better than any man I had ever known.

After a breakfast of tea and bread dipped in honey, it was time to go. Haji Sardegh walked us to the village gates and we attracted quite a crowd of followers, especially children who played around us but kept a respectful distance away from their chief. They stayed with us long after he had turned back, but eventually it was just the three of us again, walking back to the car. Having met Haji Sardegh and gained some insight into the kind of man he was, I wanted to know more about the no-go area of conversation relating to the Taliban. Hamid did his best to explain, without saying too much.

'The Taliban ruled with fear. Do you know what this is like?' he said.

'No.'

'Fear like this makes people do things they would not normally do. Haji Sardegh had a village to protect.'

'He worked with the Taliban?'

'He had no choice. They would have killed his people,' said Hamid.

'Then who is this other "chief"?'

'Someone who should have disappeared when the American planes dropped their bombs . . .'

His voice tailed away, but it began to become clear what was going on. The other chief was a Taliban supporter who had stayed on. Somewhere deep within the heart of the village a battle for control was still being waged, which might have explained Haji Sardegh's preference for wearing white, when the colour chosen by the Taliban was known to be a sombre black.

It was proof of the rumours whispered in some circles that the Taliban had not completely left Afghanistan. More worrying was the idea that they were simply waiting in the wings for reinforcements.

The notion of a Taliban uprising while I was still in Afghanistan was put to one side in favour of a different problem altogether. In other words, how to make sure your car is scorpion-free. Fortunately there was something about scorpions I didn't know, but which Abdul Latiff did. From Haji Sardegh he had acquired a unique device that consisted of two pieces of bamboo spliced loosely together. When the two pieces were rubbed against each other they apparently made a peculiar vibrating sound.

I listened.

'I can't hear anything,' I said.

'You are not a scorpion,' smiled Abdul Latiff.

The sound was said to be similar to the noises made by a territorially challenged scorpion with an anger management problem. The theory was that any real scorpion in the vicinity would evacuate at speed once he had heard it.

While Hamid and I sat on a rock at the side of the road, Abdul Latiff crawled through the car rubbing his sticks together in a furious fashion.

'Don't get bitten,' warned Hamid. 'The hospital is a long way from here.'

'Do they treat many scorpion bites at the hospital?' I asked.

Hamid shrugged.

'I do not know. I do not like spending much time there.'

He frowned slightly, as if I had reminded him of something he would rather not think about.

Instead, I tried to picture a scorpion quaking in his boots as he packed his bags in a hurry and made for the door. I wondered whether our scorpion might shape up for a fight instead, in which case Abdul Latiff was going to get a nasty surprise. But the entire exercise was thwarted when the anti-scorpion device snapped in his fingers.

I wandered over to the car and peered through the window. There were no signs of our poisonous friend evacuating, but there was a *patou*, the ubiquitous Afghan blanket crumpled up on the back seat. It occurred to me that if I was a scorpion I'd find a blanket a pretty nice place to curl up inside on a cold night. In fact I knew this to be the case because I'd read somewhere that more people in this part of the world were bitten by scorpions as they were getting into bed than at any other time.

I gingerly picked up a corner of the *patou* and dragged it outside. Sure enough, there he was, or she for that matter, tail up, stinger at the ready and looking none too pleased. With a little persuasion it left the blanket and scuttled off backwards to hide under a rock, no doubt hurling scorpion obscenities in our direction.

May your poison turn to water! May your sting lose its bite! May all your children be cross-eyed!

Scorpions are the Mike Tysons of the animal world. They just love a fight.

Before returning to Herat I persuaded Abdul Latiff to take a detour towards the mountains. He agreed reluctantly, explaining that it would be easier in a 4WD vehicle and not a typical family sedan, even though his car had been raised half a foot higher than normal to help deal with fording streams. In the end we found a reasonable path that looked as though it was used regularly by horse and cart. It was smooth and only mildly rutted in places so we made quick time to the foothills, passing the occasional nomad encampment of black tents, like upturned boats in a sea of brown. Women and children ran for cover as we came close, leaving only the menfolk to wave as we went by.

On one occasion, the wave turned to an invitation to join them for *chai sabze*, the refreshing green tea made from herbs found on the mountain slopes. It was gratefully accepted.

The nomads were lean and weather-beaten with hard mouths where the skin had stretched tight across their faces. They wore the typically baggy *shalwar* trousers and long *camise* shirt, as well as the usual *wastcot* or waistcoat that the Afghans had inherited from Victorian England during the days of Empire. However, their clothes were patched and dirty and the children were all barefoot.

The women were more colourfully clad in bright dresses adorned with a multitude of pretty trinkets and beads of glass. The little girls also wore small triangular pendants round their necks, inside which were pieces of the *Koran* to keep them safe.

A dog, its back bristling angrily, started barking at us until a small boy picked up a stone and let loose a perfectly aimed shot at its flanks. The animal yipped and slunk away with its head below its shoulders, past a goat tied to a stake that poured salt into its wounds by head-butting the poor animal in the same place.

The headman took us into his tent and we sat cross-legged on a carpet that was most probably hand-made by his forefathers. The colours and geometric patterns reminded me of a piece I had seen in the carpet museum in Tehran. That example bore a card dating it to the 17th century.

For our pleasure, and no doubt to impress us also, the headman's son appeared carrying a large copy of the holy *Koran* wrapped in silk. He crouched down and began chanting the *suras*, rocking back and forth as the words flew from his lips. At one stage he stumbled and had to start again, attracting a stern look from his father. It was then I noticed the knife on the inside of his *wastcot*. Ornate and highly sculptured, it was obviously there for more than just show.

Once the headman learned we were heading towards the mountains so that I might walk again in their shadow, he was adamant we do so from his encampment. The road worsened considerably further on, he said, and there was also still the risk of mines in these areas. Besides, the direct route was straight up following a path that was clearly visible from outside. It wound up over the hills and disappeared over a ridge before appearing again on the steeper slopes. His flock of fat-tailed sheep were up there at this moment being watched over by another of his children. We would go and bring them down for the night.

Hamid and Abdul Latiff were hesitant. They wanted to get back and anyway, their shoes were not made for mountain walking. I suggested they return to Herat and that I would find my own way back, which brought a universal cry of concern from both of them.

The situation was resolved once more by the headman. He himself would show me the way in the morning.

'Tamam,' he said, clapping his hands together to signal that there was no need for further discussion.

I watched the car recede from view as the headman started off up the track. He was a man in his late fifties but he set a cracking pace from the front and talked the whole way, only bits of which I understood. It was hard not seeing his face and eyes, which I used often to help in the translation. There are subtle nuances that can be discerned by this method; little hints that we use every day but are probably unaware of. For me, the ability to read these had grown more apparent, in the same way that a man deprived of one sense finds that the power of another becomes even more acute.

Having said that, once I had figured out the gist of the topic, it was easier to work out the related statements.

'Where are you from?' led on to 'Do you have a family?', which in turn progressed to 'How many children do you have?' and whether they were boys or girls.

Because of this the time passed quickly and before long it seemed we were high up and some distance from the tents. They appeared down below as small black dots with curls of woodsmoke rising up from the cooking fires, and with my eye I could follow the road that led back towards Pashtun Zargon.

Once more I was beset with *déjà vu*. Long ago I had walked this way. There had been the sadness of encountering the elderly woman being carried in a wheelbarrow by her grandson. She had stepped on a mine and was in a bad way, but there was nothing I or my travelling companion, Abdul Muhammad, could have done at the time. We had carried on, offering only our prayers to help speed their journey.

Not far over these same mountains we had met Aziz, the strange old man who spoke French and lived on his own in the mountains of the Qasa Murgh. It was he who had performed a 'faith healing' operation on the back of Abdul Muhammad. Successfully, I might add, because in the morning he was 'like a man released from the very shackles of gravity', as I described it at the time.

It had been slightly surreal to experience such a thing in a place like Afghanistan, but then in hindsight it was also perfectly natural. In the absence of modern medicine, obviously the old ways would still be in use.

I asked the headman whether he had heard of Aziz and he stopped in his tracks.

'Yes, yes,' he said excitedly. 'The Doktor.' And he pointed up and over the ridge in front of us, before indicating to his stomach and groaning with pain.

'*Injah*! *Khelli meriz*!'

Then he described in both words and actions what Aziz had done. The headman placed his open hand a few inches from his stomach and moved it around, as if he was massaging the air. Then he said the word *garrm* several times, which means 'warm'. After this short demonstration, he was smiling again like a man ten years younger.

This matched perfectly what I had seen Aziz do to Abdul Muhammad. It was incredible, but after all this time, the Doktor was still at large.

By mid-afternoon we had come up into a narrow valley that rose steeply, then levelled out into a wide bowl-like plateau just below the first mountain ridge. Sheep were grazing on fresh green grass and a boy with a long stick in his hands was sitting down amongst them.

It was an incredibly peaceful scene. This hidden plateau had a Shangri-La feel, a hideaway that would be a cool retreat in the summer months when the baking heat arrived down below. But now there was just the faintest edge to the air, a crisp coolness that warned of things to come. In a month, maybe two, the first cold snap would come down from the north-east and bring with it the chance of snow that would bury the feeding grounds and freeze the water supply. Although by then the headman and his tribe would be long gone. They would wait out the winter in the south towards Farah province, or even as far as Helmand.

By late afternoon we were walking back down the track pushing the flapping behinds of the fat-tailed flock before us with much hooting and hollering. I joined in and made my own racket until hoarse from the exertion. I was a fairly pathetic shepherd it has to be said. Given charge of bringing into line one particularly obstinate beast who had wandered off, I summoned every fearsome bone in my body to frighten the animal back to the flock, but it merely looked at me and continued chewing. I grabbed it by its woolly back and attempted to propel it in the desired direction, but a fat-tailed sheep is no lightweight and if there is such a noise as a sheep's laugh, I was pretty sure mine was making it.

Finally, I resorted to a different form of coercion. Collecting as much delicious grass and the odd flower as was available, I waved it in front of its nose and got the right reaction. It was certainly a sight to behold for the headman and his boy. Me, backing my way down the hill, enticing the animal with a posy of grasses and saying, 'Good sheep, nice sheep.'

Sometimes you've just got to laugh at yourself.

Hours later we had the flock safely down below, ready to be clipped one last time before winter, so that the wool could be turned into thread to make items of clothing for the tribe, or for sale in the markets.

The women had cooked some meat over an open fire near the headman's tent and the smell wafted inside to where we were seated in a circle. Bread wrapped in a cloth was also procured from a carpet-bag hanging in the corner. There was the headman and his two sons, another much older man who was almost blind from glaucoma and two others about my age who I hadn't seen before. The women also joined us for the meal, but formed their own circle outside of ours.

I kept catching the eye of the youngest, who would flash a smile and then look away, prompting a chorus of giggles from the group. She was a pretty woman of about nineteen and her eyes were dark and beautiful, accentuated by the use of some kind of eye-liner that made them seem even larger. There were coloured bracelets on her wrists and rings on her fingers, which was how all the women wore their wealth. It was a way of communicating social stature as well as attracting a mate, and from the looks I was getting it was the latter rather than the former that was being suggested. In Islam more than one wife is permitted, but I could just imagine the reaction at home when I arrived back with someone else in tow.

'Libby, meet Zahra. Now, if you would just put down

the knife we can maybe sort this out.'

Of course nothing was about to happen. Not in a tent with five snoring men, I assumed. But how wrong I was when the time came to turn off the oil light that flickered from its hook halfway up the pole.

I was taken to another tent a short distance away and shown where I was to sleep. There was a long-haired rug spread out on the floor and a roll of carpet as a pillow. A softer quilt of some kind was also neatly folded nearby to ward off the cold night air, although I knew I would have no trouble sleeping. The walk in the mountains had seen to that. Within minutes of lying down I must have dozed off, only to be woken again by a noise outside the tent. I thought of the dog, or that bloody sheep come back to taunt me, but no. When the flap folded back, there was the young woman standing in the light of the moon that had just risen. The reason for her presence was immediately obvious. She was an offering, but one that I knew would get me into a whole lot of trouble. In the morning I would be as good as married, or dead. Whichever, I was going to be killed anyway when my wife found out. So I was left with a tricky decision; how to get her out of the tent without either offending her or risking insulting the headman and his family. The possibility of pretending to be asleep was ruled out when she slipped under the cover beside me. I was now looking into a very pretty pair of eyes that could see quite clearly I was awake. There was a scent of perfume also. It was difficult to tell, but the warmth emanating from her body suggested she wasn't wearing anything either.

'*Nah lutfen. Rafteed,*' I said quietly, urging her politely to go.

She giggled softly, either because of my elementary (and possibly incorrect) Farsi or something else.

'*Mahn,*' she said, pointing at herself.

'*Belli,*' I nodded.

At this she slowly rose up and stood over me, naked in the dim light. I heard the sound of her bracelets clinking. She was indeed very lovely.

'*Mahn?*' she said again, pointing at herself once more.

I must have replied, though I don't remember saying anything, because she wrapped herself in her cloak and walked out into the night.

116

22

In the morning there was no one about. The sun was not yet up and it was cold, but I was wide awake and troubled by what to do next. Wait for the headman to accuse me of deflowering his daughter, or of refusing her?

I decided to start walking. I ambled off as one might when they are just going for a stroll, then the further I went the faster my step became. I was feeling progressively better when from behind me there was a shout and I looked around to see the headman waving.

'Bugger!' I said.

There was a rustle of hooves over by some rocks and my ears were filled with the haughty cackle of sheep.

Making my way back I was encouraged to see he wasn't holding a gun, and that the knife in his waistcoat was still where it should be. He was smiling too which was also a good sign.

'*Koojah mireed*?' he asked.

'Just walking,' I replied guiltily. Then I made it seem as though I was looking for somewhere to ablute, and he pointed me to a narrow gully in the opposite direction. It was littered with stones which supplanted the need for toilet paper. There was also a stream trickling out from under a large boulder in which I could wash.

Afterwards I was invited in for breakfast, but there was neither mention nor sign of the girl. We ate bread and a cheese made from sheep's milk, drank hot tea and then departed in the direction of Herat. I had survived. But only just.

The walk was long and took the whole day. We followed the line of the mountain range until the minarets of Herat came into view on our right. Then it was simply a case of heading over the open, undulating ground towards them. At this point the headman bade farewell, having brought me to a point where I couldn't get lost, and I thanked him for his hospitality – mindful of how great it had almost been. He smiled for perhaps a little longer than was necessary, then I set out to cover the remaining twenty or so kilometres to the city.

From time to time the minarets would disappear as I wandered down into a dry river-bed or gully, but always they would re-emerge to guide me. At first it was easy, but as I descended down towards the Hari Rud, I realised I would no longer be able to see them. Herat was still a long way off and at this low level, even the tallest minaret would be hidden.

However, by the afternoon, having reached the river and waded across its freezing cold waters at the shallowest point, I knew that with the sun on my face the city would reveal itself eventually. And that is exactly what it did.

Just as late afternoon was turning to early evening I found myself walking along one of the banks of the river when a broad road appeared. It was wide and straight, and led up a slight incline to what looked to be some buildings.

Further on the buildings turned into stores and small work-shops where boys were busily restoring old generators. Wearily I trudged the rest of the way into the city, passing through busy marketplaces and narrow lanes filled with spice sellers, before coming across the old fort which towered over everything. From there it was just a short walk to the hotel and when the stench of the open sewer reached me, I knew that I was home.

There was something new in the air, however: the smell of smoke. Somewhere in Herat a fire was burning.

That night in the hotel's restaurant I ran into the inimitable Ghollum Sefarr again and he invited me to join him at his table.

It was his last night before returning to Kabul – not with the trucks, but by light aeroplane.

'Did you find your friend?' he asked.

'Not yet.'

'If you wish I can ask some of my people if they have heard of him.'

'In Kabul?'

'No, here in Herat. Some of the drivers are Herati. Perhaps they will know something. As you realise, we have no telephone books. The only way to find someone is the old-fashioned way. But I will tell you this. Afghans are not normally suspicious people, but these days it is a fact of life. You have to be careful. Understand?'

'I think so.'

'Just remember if you ask an Afghan, "Where is so-and-so?" they may know the answer but they will say they don't. Unless you are a friend or family, that is different – but you, you are a stranger and they will think maybe you are CIA or something.'

Immediately the events at Pashtun Zargon sprang back into mind, and the caginess of a certain Haji Sardegh. These were troubled times and not everyone was who they made out to be.

'How about you?' I asked. 'Are you CIA?'

Ghollum Sefarr thought this was the funniest thing he had ever heard. He practically fell off his chair laughing, so much so that the cook in the kitchen popped his head round the corner to see what was going on. He wiped his hands on a greasy towel and spat impressively, then went back inside to empty the contents of his nasal cavities hopefully into a sink rather than the soup.

Ghollum Sefarr was still shaking his head and chuckling, but he never did reply to the question. Instead he changed the subject to the political situation in his country and the changing face of world affairs.

'You know, Karzai is a good man.'

'The Afghan President?'

'Yes. Even though he is still a Pathan, he is a moderate one.'

Mention of the Pathan (or Pashtun people) raised the question of Afghanistan's continuing problems with tribal conflict. The Pathan were a minority but held all the top governmental posts.

They were said to regard the others – Tadjiks, Hazars and the rest – as the great unwashed, good for menial labour while actual control of the country was best left in their hands. Indeed, they had made their language the language of politics and bureaucracy, which meant you had to speak Pashtu to have any chance of gaining a position in the game.

'It is a very difficult language,' said Ghollum Sefarr. 'The grammar, actually, it is a lot like English.'

'English?'

'Well, you must remember the English have been in this area for a long time. They introduced the political structures we inherited.'

'And do they work?'

'Do they work in England?' he questioned.

'Point taken,' I said.

We ate in silence for a while, chewing the tough meat and shovelling great heaps of rice into our mouths with pieces of flat bread. It was better to use the bread, because you never knew where the knives and forks had been.

It seemed that it was a night for deep and philosophical conversation which was good because it kept my mind off the girl in the tent.

'The Internet is not good,' he said. Ghollum Sefarr was prone to leaping into topics with bold statements.

'Why is that?' I replied.

'All the sexing.'

'You mean pornography?'

'Yes, sexing. Men and women with no decency.'

Suddenly I was back in the tent again.

He continued, 'At the office in Kabul there is a man and he is always looking at the pictures on the computer. He says, "Ghollum Sefarr, come and look at this!" I look and I can't believe my eyes. I don't want to look any more.'

'That's a problem.'

'Big problem,' he said through a mouthful of rice.

23

The next day the kites were dancing a merry jig above the power lines in Herat, kept aloft by the heat from the city rising into the air and through the efforts of the children whose method it was to constantly tug at the strings, urging their home-made flying inventions higher and higher. Occasionally a gust of wind would send their kites soaring, or it would have the opposite effect, leaving them crumpled and broken on the ground, such was the extremely delicate nature of their construction. None of these kites had tails either, which was presumably to lighten the load even further. It seemed everything in the country was minimised to the barest level necessary for operation, even the people, who existed on meagre rations of bread, meat, rice and fruit – although the fruit amounted to small blackened bananas and the odd blighted apple.

It was a diet I was used to from the time before in Afghanistan when we augmented our food supplies by raiding derelict orchards of mulberry trees, ever fearful that a sniper might see us, and I was rapidly beginning to feel the effects of a much reduced consumption. I'd already pulled my belt in another notch and my clothes had a baggy feeling that was not there at the outset. I was also walking many miles each and every day, so by seven-thirty or eight o'clock at night I was asleep, ready to wake before dawn the next morning.

It was a fantastic feeling. Here, life was pared back to only what was necessary, and as a result I was much better for it. An old feeling of balance and strength was returning, unfettered by office politics or stress, and like the kites above the city I was enjoying the sense of freedom that came with it.

It was after the long walk from the mountains that I stumbled across Hamid walking out of the hospital. He stopped when he saw me and I saw the look on his face brighten artificially, as if he was hiding something he'd rather I didn't see.

'You are well?' I enquired.

'I am fine,' he replied, then he habitually flung his *patou* over his shoulder before starting off in the direction of the hotel. We walked on in silence, passing an elderly woman sitting on the pavement with her hand upraised in the air, begging for money. Hamid took out a roll of notes and peeled off a few hundred rupiyeh before pressing them into her palm. I did the same and her eyes never looked up, though she muttered her thanks to Allah, as if the money had come from heaven rather than from mortal hands.

I caught up to Hamid again. He walked with his hands clasped behind his back and his head down.

'What's wrong?' I asked. 'I thought you didn't like hospitals.'

'I don't,' he said, but instead of offering anything more in the way of an explanation, he stayed silent. I tried one more time to prise him out of his reluctant mood. I told him I hated hospitals as well, ever since my father became ill when I was young and he was forced to stay several nights for tests that somehow managed to miss the cancer spreading throughout his body. I hated the white sheets and the smell of disinfectant, the echoing corridors and the panic-squeak of rubber soles on linoleum. They were not natural places for me, not somewhere that I felt my father belonged. I still felt if we could get him back to the water's edge, it was his beloved sea that would make him well again.

'You can swim?' he asked.

I nodded.

He added, 'In the ocean?'

'Of course,' I said. I described my home for him and he was amazed that such a life existed.

'I always thought,' he said, 'that the sea was a terrible place. I saw the movie *Titanic* and it was cold. People died.'

I noticed him give a furtive look over his shoulder at the hospital.

'So you have someone in there,' I said, nodding towards the building. He looked at me as if he was deciding what to say. Eventually, however, perhaps because we had built up a level of trust over recent days, he started to talk.

'My sister is sick, but the doctors can't tell us why because they don't have the right machine. There is one in Islamabad but that is too far and we don't have the money. She has headaches that last for days and she is not herself sometimes.'

He sighed.

'So you think sea water might help?' he asked suddenly.

I wanted to be able to say yes, but the truth was I never had the chance to find out for sure.

'Then,' he said, 'what we need is some kind of a miracle.'

Oddly enough, moments later out of a clear blue sky that showed not a single cloud, it began to snow.

24

I looked at my shoulders and they were already developing a layer of white. Hamid too had white flecks in his hair and beard. But on closer inspection we soon realised it was ash, not snow, that was falling. I looked up and it was swirling above us and landing on everything: the trees, the cars, the people. A small child was sitting nearby shrieking with fear, until the blue sail-like figure of a woman bustled past and swept him up into her arms.

All Hamid had to say was, 'Come. You must see this.'

He led me down the road, walking quickly now as if we might be late for something important. Soon I could see trucks being unloaded and a group of people standing on the footpath watching silently.

'It is the bank,' he said, breaking into a run. 'They are burning the money!'

I have never seen such a sight before and I very much doubt if I ever will again. Huge quantities of cash were being thrown into two-metre-high earthen incinerators in an open yard near the Bank of Afghanistan. There was just a low wall, no more than chest high, separating us from the vast wealth being rapidly consumed by the flames, although an armed guard with a big bushy beard and narrow-set eyes watched sullenly from his vantage point standing on the wall. With every load of money thrown in there would be a sudden *whoomph* and the flames would reach up even higher, sending partially burnt notes flying into the air. They were ruined, still burning as they floated on the updrafts, but this didn't stop the poor, the hungry and the downright optimistic amongst the crowd from chasing them down in the hope that something might be rescued from the inferno. Many were beggars and it seemed so cruel that the authorities would do this in the public domain. The ashes of a massive fortune were falling on their shoulders, reminding them of what they did not and would probably never own.

I found Hamid and asked him to explain why it was all happening.

'It is the old money,' he said. 'Now they are printing new notes which will be harder to copy.'

It was a harmless enough statement, but of course alluded to another of the problems facing Afghanistan. A secure economy would first require a secure form of currency. The old money had been printed in Pakistan decades ago and, while it was all the people had to deal with, no one totally trusted it.

'In Pakistan,' said Hamid, 'you can buy colour photocopy machines so that you print your own money.'

He shrugged his usual Eeyore sort of shrug and turned back to the show over the wall.

The men whose job it was to feed the flames were beginning to wilt under the heat. At first they had been using their hands, but now a wheelbarrow was found to ease their burden. They would run at the incinerator along an adjoining platform and stopping just short of the edge, up would go the wheelbarrow, down would go the money, and then they would retreat backwards using the barrow as a shield. It worked well for the first few goes until one man forgot to hold on and the wheel-barrow itself was consumed by the fire. The crowd laughed and cheered, though some took this opportunity to climb up onto the wall to get a better look. Immediately the guard waved his gun and gesticulated vehemently at the offenders, who took little notice until he fired a few rounds menacingly into the air. An ugly situation was averted for the time being, but obviously this one guard would never be enough to control the mass of people watching if they decided to take matters into their own hands.

I managed to take a few shots with my camera, but the last

one caught the guard's attention and he was soon standing over me, pointing at the camera and indicating that I should give it to him. I refused, of course, and told him I was not with any press agency, but that I was merely a traveller. Hamid also lent a few words of his own to back me up and when some others decided to take up my cause, the guard was outnumbered. I put the camera away in my canvas shoulder-bag and watched as he went off to patrol another part of his wall.

He was the sole finger in the dyke, holding back a flood of poverty, but the finger was also on the trigger and you could tell he wasn't in the mood to take prisoners. The dam stayed intact this time and the rest of the money went up in smoke.

Hamid and I made our way back to the hotel in a shower of useless currency. The thought of his sister in the hospital without the necessary medicine to make her well again started me thinking. What if Ghollum Sefarr could help with his contacts in the Italian Embassy? Perhaps there would be a way of getting Hamid's sister to whatever piece of equipment she needed. Was it so far-fetched an idea? At least it was worth a try.

Some time later I tracked down the man in question who was unpacking his bags in his room. The trucks were delayed another day on the border because the Iranian authorities demanded to search the convoy thoroughly, which meant they wanted to see whatever they could pilfer in the name of the Islamic Republic. Ghollum Sefarr was, however, still smiling.

'Mr CIA,' he said jokingly as I pushed open his door.

'Cut it out. Walls have ears, remember.'

Ghollum Sefarr stood up and glanced at the wall behind his bed. It was a whitewashed wall with brown stains of damp in the corner. Someone had written a few lines of Farsi near the bed-head and then tried to wipe them out, leaving an even more prominent, inky smudge. But of ears Ghollum Sefarr could see none.

'It's an expression,' I said. 'Dating back to the Second World War.'

'Teach me this expression, please. What does it mean?'

'It means be careful because people on the other side of the wall might be listening.'

'Ah yes, it's a good one. Please write it down for me in this.'

He picked up a notebook from his bedside table and opened it to the back page where there were many other sayings and proverbs in English and some in Italian. As I wrote, I asked him about the chances of him helping Hamid's sister.

He arched his head back and scratched the front of his neck near the Adam's apple.

'What can I do?' he said finally.

'That is what I am asking. What can you do?'

'Nothing.'

He placed one hand on his heart. 'I would like to help. Yes, of course, but what you are asking is beyond me and probably anyone. I can tell you now the Embassy will not get involved in aiding an Afghan woman. News would get out and there would be a thousand Afghan women, ten thousand wanting the same help. I know Hamid, he is a good boy, but . . .'

He put his hands in the air in resignation.

'It is easier for you to help her than for me,' he said.

Just then his satellite phone started ringing and by the look on his face the news wasn't good. I walked out of his room and left him with his own problems. Mine, however, had only just begun. Having started something I was now honour-bound to finish it. Money alone would not solve anything. It might get her to Islamabad if she had a passport, which was unlikely, but the difficulties associated with receiving the right treatment once there seemed enormous.

There was another solution. It was a complete wild shot, an act of utter craziness, but because of that it had every chance of working.

25

Hamid listened to my idea with some scepticism. He sat on the edge of his chair in the hotel office and with practised ease flicked a string of prayer beads through his fingers.

'You know this Doktor?' he said.

'I have met him. It was a while ago, but he still lives not far from Pashtun Zargon. About three days' walk.'

'My sister could never get that far.'

'Well, what I'm hoping is that she won't have to. If I can organise it, Abdul Latiff will bring Aziz here to the hospital.'

'I don't know,' he said.

It was clear the health of his sister weighed heavily upon him. It was a responsibility that had fallen on his shoulders, not only as the eldest son but as the breadwinner for his family as well. I knew already from past conversations that he had lost his father in the war, courtesy of a Russian bullet.

'So how do you contact this Aziz?' he asked.

'By letter, which you will help me write.'

'And he will remember you?'

'I think so, yes. I'm sure he will.'

The letter was composed on a single blank piece of paper, torn from my journal. It described me, as I was in 1989, and the circumstances in which we had met each other, Abdul Muhammad, his back and the remarkable recovery he had made. There was also a potted history of Aziz's life, told to me in his own words as we sat outside his house in the valley.

Aziz was an Afghan who had travelled widely in his youth, particularly to France. In 1946 he had journeyed to Paris, carrying only a copy of Gautier's *Les Jeunes-France*. Finding work in a printer's shop he had stayed many years, living and working – even loving – in Montparnasse. It had been the time of his life, but after ten years there had been trouble – he never told me what kind – and he had been forced to leave for Marseilles.

But Marseilles was not Paris and his time in France had drawn to an end. Eventually, returning to Afghanistan, he set up his own printing business and settled down with a wife and family. But the war came and tragedy with it. Both his wife and only child were killed in the early years, forcing him to give up his life in Herat and retire to the mountains.

In the letter were also a few words that I hoped would help jog Aziz's memory, if all else failed. It was something he had said to me on the day of my departure from his home in the valley: a reference to me being in Paris when 'he would see it again through my eyes'. At the time it was strange, most notably because I was heading in the opposite direction. In fact, Paris could not have been further from my mind.

But Aziz seemed to know something that I did not. In time I did make it to Paris, in the springtime when the blossoms were a parade of colour along the banks of the Seine, and met my future wife in the garden of Rodin's museum.

Finally, the letter explained the ailment inflicting Hamid's sister, which he himself detailed, and a request for help. If Aziz was willing and able, transportation from Pashtun Zargon would be arranged. The letter was sealed and on the front of the envelope Hamid wrote in Farsi: *Doktor Aziz. Qasa Murgh.*

'So now what happens?' said Hamid.

'Ask Abdul Latiff to deliver this to the headman we met in the mountains. He will know what to do.'

It was like a play in which the scriptwriter has elevated the level of suspense so that no one dare leave to go to the bathroom in case a vital clue is missed. Only in this case there was no telling how the whole story was going to pan out. If Aziz was going to become a part of the plot, then it would take some doing. In 1989 he was an old man. In 2003 there was a chance he might be too frail to make such a journey. But at the very least we had tried.

That night I attended an English class in a small room with concrete floors and three rows of desks at the rear, facing an old-fashioned blackboard at the front. There were less than a dozen students, all of whom were like Hamid in that they sought to improve their English in order to get better jobs. One young man was a doctor with Médecin Sans Frontières, another an engineer whose work with the international relief groups was being frustrated by his command of the language. Then there was Hamid, who wanted to be a journalist one day.

I sat at the back and was acknowledged by the teacher, a young man no older than his students. He had apparently already had word there would be a 'native speaker' in his class and it seemed to be making him quite nervous.

'Welcome to our friend,' he said in a loud, slightly quavering voice, indicating me and then speaking more softly, 'Your name is please?'

'My name is Richard Loseby.'

His voice went back to loudspeaker volume.

'Thank you, you see class . . .'

He picked up a piece of chalk and wrote in large letters on the blackboard: MY NAME IS RICHARD.

'This is the correct method of introduction, not "I am called Richard". We say "The animal is called a . . ."'

He looked at me expectantly and I blurted out the first thing that came to mind.

'Sheep.'

'Yes, the animal is called a sheep. Say after me: "My name is Richard. The animal is called a sheep."'

The class chanted obediently which had Hamid suppressing a fit of the giggles.

'Good,' said the teacher, who was looking at me again. 'Can you tell us what is the plural form of sheep please?'

'Sheep,' I said.

'Yes, what is the plural form we should use for this animal?'

'Sheep,' I repeated. 'It's the same. One sheep, two sheep.'

I was beginning to wish I had thought of something easier

like 'hairy mammoth' or 'Ecuadorean ring-tailed opossum'.

The young doctor in front of me turned around.

'Why not sheeps?' he asked.

'I don't know.'

'What is your job please?'

'I'm a writer.'

He looked genuinely surprised.

'You are a writer and you don't know English?'

'It's not that, it's just, well . . . um . . .'

Happily the teacher jumped in at that point and took control of the class again. Normality resumed and the lesson went on to cover the many nuances of the English language, from first person participles to the correct use of the semi-colon. It was a relief that 'sheep' was not mentioned again.

After the class was over, we were making our way down the stairs to the street when a hand touched my shoulder. It was one of the students who had stayed silent for the entire lesson, presumably because his English was not as good as the others and he did not want to embarrass himself. However, his abilities were exactly the opposite.

Ali was a finely spoken young Afghan in his early twenties with a clean-shaven, strong-jawed face. His skin also was perfect, not a pimple or blemish anywhere, and he had combed his black hair back in a rakish fashion so that he resembled a sort of Afghan Marlon Brando.

As it so happened, Ali did have a connection with the movie world. His father used to run the old cinema in Herat, which had outlasted the Russians but not the Taliban. His youth was a mixture of Hollywood and Bolliwood – Sylvester Stallone and Sanjeev Kumar – but it was the black-and-white American classics that were his fond favourite. He did a half-decent James Cagney imitation as we walked along one of the main streets towards the 800-year-old Masjid-i-Juma, or Friday Mosque, causing an elderly man on a bicycle to almost fall off.

It was after the evening prayer, so the mosque was quiet and almost empty of people. From a corner of the vast central courtyard a voice was 'singing' in prayer, chanting verses from the *Koran* that were mesmerizing. A few men were gathered in the middle, but they paid us no attention. We carried our shoes across the ancient flagstones and sat under one of the *ivans* on the northern side, surrounded by ceramic tiles of azure blue that carried the conspicuous vertical and oblique strokes of Arabic script, with the more rounded Persian script contained beneath it. Ali pointed out a poem of penitence by the 12th-century Persian poet Attar.

'There are many things the Taliban destroyed in their time here,' he said. 'My father's cinema was the first to go. They turned it into a mosque, but nothing so great as this one.'

He was right. The Masjid-i-Juma was a special place which, perhaps unlike other architecturally superior mosques in Mashad, was not a magnet for millions of pilgrims and therefore had retained a sense of peace. It was a place to go to escape the world beyond its walls, and this explained why Ali was a regular visitor outside the normal prayer times.

'You don't come here to pray then?' I said.

'Sometimes, more now than when the Taliban forced us to come and beat us with sticks if we did not. Because of the cinema my father and I were singled out.'

Just then a stray cat appeared at a door nearby and was shooed out by a man with a walking stick. The cat received a clout about the hindquarters and ran off at speed.

'We're alike, me and cat. A pair of poor nameless slobs,' said Ali suddenly.

'What's that?'

'*Breakfast at Tiffany's*. Holly Golightly. It's just a line from the movie. Have you seen it?'

'Several times, usually on rainy weekends.'

'I like the old movies. Life was much less complicated then.'

He chuckled at a sudden thought, still looking at the huge wooden doors through which the cat had made a hasty exit.

'It should take you four seconds to walk out that door. I'll give you two.'

I looked at him quizzically.

'Same film,' he said with a smile. 'Same actress.'

The stories that Ali was able to tell me of life under the Taliban rule were fascinating at the same time as they were horrifying. Herat was a city with a proud artistic and literary history that dated back centuries. Some of the finest writers, poets and thinkers had come from this area of Afghanistan. And yet this creative freedom had been firmly quashed by the Pashtun-speaking Taliban, most of whom were just young people from the border areas of Pakistan with little more education than rote learning of the *Koran*.

But Ali also spoke of the resistance that was offered by those unwilling to give up completely. There were many, he said, within literary circles who mocked the Taliban by circulating defamatory poems and verse.

'It went over their heads most of the time,' he said wryly.

Herati authors often used the two-verse, four-sentence poem known as '*dobaiti*', or the comic essays called '*tanz*' to ridicule their dim-witted persecutors. The one time there was trouble was when a simple, twenty-page journal called *Aworang-i-Hashtum*, or *The Eighth Throne* – a reference to a classic book entitled *The Seventh Throne* by the 14th-century Herati author Jami – refused to publish a sermon by the Taliban leader, Mullah Omar. The publication was closed down for six months.

There were worse punishments handed down, however, when the Taliban got wise to the underground writers' movement. Jail sentences were of an indefinite length and sometimes given without trial, while public flogging was also used. One writer received eighty lashes for exposing malpractices in the Taliban-run hospital.

'He was a mess when they cut him down,' said Ali.

I asked him how life compared now that Ismail Khan was in control of Herat, and he was more positive but still not over the moon. Ismail Khan, he said, was better this time round rather than last time when he was governor before the Taliban invasion. But there were still conservative thinkers within his administration who threatened to ruin the new feeling of freedom.

'Do you think the Taliban could return?' I asked.

'It is possible, but not likely I think. Not in Herat. Ismail Khan is strong and he has his own army of men with tanks and helicopters. The city is heavily guarded, so I think the Taliban would find it difficult to return.'

I thought how easy it had been for me to walk into the city

via the river, without a checkpoint in sight, and wondered whether Ismail Khan had enough men to patrol everywhere. Ali seemed to read my mind.

'But then,' he said, 'maybe Mullah Omar is an Arnold Schwarzenegger.'

'How?'

Ali ducked his chin to his chest in theatrical fashion and dropped his voice an octave to deliver the mother of all movie lines.

'I'll be back.'

26

I t was a hot day on the way to the village of Seoshan when we came across Ismail Khan and his entourage of heavily armed 4WD vehicles.

Seoshan was one of the places where I had spent some time during the war and when Abdul Latiff had returned from delivering the letter, Hamid and I set out for this small isolated village which was about ten kilometres outside the city along a series of dusty roads.

What Ismail Khan was doing this far out was something of a mystery, but his cars were bristling with guns and travelling towards us at speed. Unfortunately, the road we were on, which was nothing more than a twin-rutted track used more by horse and cart than modern vehicles, was bordered by a high wall on one side and a deep creek on the other. The creek was over-flowing with water and in places had burst its banks to make small lakes alongside the road. There was nowhere to go to get out of the way, and Abdul Latiff was in an obstinate mood.

'You go back!' he roared at the driver in the leading vehicle. 'There is a crossroads only two hundred metres behind you!'

'Old man,' replied the driver, who must have been all of eighteen, 'we are five cars and you are only one. You go back or we will push you into the water!'

Abdul Latiff physically grew in stature.

'Old man!' he spluttered. I think he was about to punch the impudent youngster when a voice called out from the middle of the motorcade and seemed to calm things down. I caught sight of a fifty-something-year-old man with a wide beard and a barrel chest who wore a smart suit jacket over his light brown *shalwar camise*. At his barked command the line of shiny 4WDs reversed up the narrow lane to the crossroads and we passed them by like royalty, although the cars were fitted with darkened windows and it was impossible to see inside.

Abdul Latiff, however, was under no illusions.

'What about that!' he exclaimed seconds later. 'The Governor of Herat makes way for Abdul Latiff!'

He gripped the wheel and roared with laughter.

'Old man! Ha!'

We rolled into Seoshan in a shower of rain that seemed not to have come from any cloud overhead. It was very light and served only to help keep the dust down as we passed the first few houses. The road was just as narrow, barely wide enough for the car in places as we made our way through a warren of village lanes hemmed in by vertical walls on either side.

It was the smell that was immediately recognisable. Seoshan was a strongly farming village, surrounded by green fields and with many cows and goats which gave it a particularly agricultural aroma. It brought back memories of the days spent living there before the final farewell to Nebi was made. Seoshan was the last place I had seen him and it was there that he had presented me with a prized possession, the bayonet from a Russian AK47.

I still had the bayonet, tucked away in a cardboard box in a cupboard because my wife didn't like the look of it. She was right, of course, it was an instrument of war that had no doubt been used for its intended purpose, and so I had not protested. There are better things to place upon the mantelpiece than a blade stained with blood.

I was very proud of that knife all the same.

In Seoshan there was very little that had changed over the centuries, let alone since the time I was last there. Only the children who had played on the burnt-out remains of Soviet tanks were grown up and had children of their own, who played on the same ageing artillery.

A regular meeting place for all ages had been a troop carrier that was stopped by a mujahedeen RPG, or rocket-propelled grenade, just as it was trying to cross one of the irrigation ditches that went around the village. That same vehicle was still there and performing the same service as a place where people would meet to sit and talk. They stood up as we came close and directed us to the home of the village chief, not far away up a narrow path. We left the car and continued on foot until his door was reached.

As in Pashtun Zargon, the leading member of the community was a senior citizen. In Afghanistan age brings respect and authority, which helps to maintain the status quo, for good or bad. Change is not something that is welcomed with open arms. The wheat was still being threshed the old way by the hooves of oxen drawing a special kind of wooden cart with spiked wheels. Then the chaff was separated by throwing it into the air using hand-made rakes and letting the wind blow away what was not required.

In the case of Seoshan, the village leader was a grey-haired man with a rugged look about him that suggested he did more than pontificate about village affairs, he rolled up his sleeves and mucked in. He stood six feet tall in his sandals and would have been taller still but for a stoop that showed he was no spring chicken. I noticed the door to his house, although identical to its neighbours in that it was wooden and painted blue, was taller by a good few inches.

He was a congenial host who walked us through the village and listened with much interest to my stories of Seoshan. He knew well the man I had stayed with, Sufi Seqi, and sadly showed me where he was buried; a little cemetery by a stream that I thought a less than fitting place for a man who was larger than life. Sufi Seqi had a deep bass voice and an ability to use it powerfully whenever he wanted something done. He was a commander who engendered great respect, even amongst those mujahedeen like Nebi who fought for a different group.

Later I would discover that an illness had claimed his life

and not an act of war as most would have predicted.

There were other people I mentioned which brought no more than a cursory nod, neither a yes or a no in terms of recognition, including the name Mohandaspoor. Although I did learn one thing from Hamid which was interesting. 'Mohandas' meant engineer and 'poor' translated as family. So Mohandaspoor meant a 'family of engineers' and I was once again reminded of Nebi's prowess under the bonnet of the captured Russian truck. I made a mental note to follow up the lead Ghollum Sefarr had mentioned regarding his drivers. Perhaps in the trucking fraternity they might know of something?

The afternoon was spent down by the wreck of the troop carrier that was suspended across the stream. We had not been allowed to leave without joining in their conversation which, oddly enough, had raged all day on the subject of Osama bin Laden. Apparently our presence had started it. Word had got out that a foreigner was in the village looking for the world's most wanted criminal and the joke was that Osama was hiding in Mohammad's cattle pen under his house.

It was like watching a game of tennis.

Mohammad, a wiry man with bad teeth and a slightly crazy smile, was having nothing of it. Although obviously enjoying being the centre of attention, even if it was at his expense, he pointed the finger back at his accuser and claimed that there were far worse things hiding in this man's toilet that President Bush should know about.

At this the small crowd had cracked up with laughter. The game was tied at fifteen all. Everyone was waiting to see what would happen next.

The accuser returned with an angled serve to the corner. He waved away the remark about the contents of his bathroom (which I knew would be like all the others, a small hut suspended over a garden with nothing but a few stones inside to wipe yourself clean) and said that at least he had a bathroom to speak of.

Mohammad tried a drop shot by insisting his garden was larger, although this was immediately refuted by one or two in the crowd. The ball dropped short and hit the net, and when Mohammad's opponent upped the ante by counting heads of cattle and coming up one cow and two goats better than Mohammad, it was game, set and match.

Mohammad managed to laugh it off and the others clapped him on the back to show that nothing was meant, but I wouldn't be too sure that he wasn't secretly planning revenge.

The question of the whereabouts of Osama bin Laden returned with less joking and more of a sober mood. It was interesting to hear their comments, far away from those so often expressed by the international press. Here was the man on the street, speaking his mind.

'What is all the fuss with this Arab?' they asked. 'Why do the Americans want him so badly? What has he done to anger them?'

I spoke to them about the World Trade Center towers and how Osama bin Laden was being held accountable for their destruction. But of this huge moment in history they were profoundly ignorant.

'What buildings? When did this happen?'

It may seem strange to a westerner's mind, but in parts of Afghanistan they are blissfully unaware of the reason for all the interest in their country and its Al-Qaeda-friendly Taliban. To them, the military action was just something the Americans did. In fact they assumed that my own country had probably been liberated in a similar fashion.

I thought of the armies of fast-food chains and shopping malls that had long since marched across my land. Maybe they were right. The Americans had taken over, although without the use of smart bombs and helicopter gunships. They had simply sent their culture instead, a far more invasive and destructive weapon.

As to the location of Osama, the villagers of Seoshan were none the wiser and nor did it really matter to them. They had no quarrel with him. He was just one of those crazy Arabs with money.

On the way back to the city Hamid suggested we go to see

'The Inventor of Herat', a man who had devoted many years to the reconstruction of a Russian attack helicopter that had crashed nearby.

It was not long before we were getting out of the car again and looking at a brightly painted helicopter, although it was far from resembling the hi-tech killing machine it had once been. The main rotor was there and the smaller one at the rear. The cockpit had been salvaged with its primary controls in working order, but the engine had been replaced by a diesel truck engine and the entire contraption sat flush on the ground.

For our benefit the old inventor started her up and with a throaty roar the rotors began to move, slowly at first, then faster and faster. Suddenly, without much of a warning, he changed the gears and both rotors started spinning with such velocity that the entire machine threatened to take off without anyone seated at the controls. The noise was enormous, as was the risk. If something were to work itself loose we would all be killed.

Fortunately, and perhaps because the situation was getting just a bit out of hand, he hit a switch and the engine promptly died. The incredible flying machine settled back down to earth and resumed the appearance of a piece of '70s artwork.

'I thought it was going to take off for a minute,' I said to Hamid.

He repeated my comment to the old inventor, who smiled and tapped a steel cable that tied the helicopter to a post in the ground.

One day this thing was going to kill someone, I thought. Then it occurred to me that perhaps in its original state it already had.

27

That night Abdul Latiff invited us both to his house for dinner. He lived in a typical narrow street with high walls on either side. In the wires overhead, the tattered remains of small kites were hanging like washing. Children of all ages played in the dirt of the road even though it was approaching dark, and everything was surrounded by the incessant hum of a large generator that powered the neighbourhood.

Hamid and I waited in the road while Abdul Latiff went through his iron gate in the wall and informed his wife there would be guests. I wondered if the response would be as one might expect at home.

'Hon, a few of the guys from the office have come round for dinner!'

'What! But we have nothing in the freezer, the kids are still in the bath and I look like a wreck.'

Perhaps not, because within a few seconds we were ushered through a small courtyard and into his home. There were two rooms connected to each other through a wide Islamic-style arch, but both were similarly decorated with Persian and Afghan rugs on the floor and pillows also made of rugs to rest against. A recess in one of the walls held all the blankets and beds which were rolled up each morning and tucked away.

The most prominent feature was a large television in a wooden cabinet at the far end of the second room, which was visible from the first. Clearly the western media had paid well during their time in Herat because when the TV was turned on Abdul Latiff started flicking through a number of satellite channels. Even the normally unflappable Hamid was impressed; not many people could afford satellite, though he didn't say anything.

Next door to the hotel was an electrical appliance store that was stocked with everything you might expect to find in any western shop: fridges, PlayStations, toasters, clocks that reminded you of the correct prayer times, stereos and satellite dishes, but these were usually the playthings of the international community working in the area, and of the rich warlords who had made a tidy sum from either the gun business, the drug business or both.

We sat for a while in silence and watched the news on BBC World. Then came a programme about cars that featured the latest Lamborghini, or 'Lambo' as the announcer preferred to call it. Over a quarter of a million dollars of metal that accelerated round the purpose-built track like a jet fighter. It was hugely ironic, of course, to be sitting in such humble surroundings, eating a simple meal of rice and chicken, while in the background a very English voice waxed lyrical about something that only an infinitesimal fraction of the world's population could afford. It was the supreme example of wealth – Mammon's own motorcar – though this didn't stop the three of us staying glued to the set the entire time.

When it was over, Abdul Latiff's children arrived from the kitchen where they had eaten their own meal. It was situated to one side of the courtyard and separated from the two rooms we occupied. There were three boys ranging from nine down to just one. I made a comment to Hamid that Abdul Latiff had started a family late in life compared to most. The reason, of course, was the war.

'Abdul Latiff spent a long time in prison after he was captured by the Russians,' he said.

'How long?'

Hamid checked with Abdul Latiff as his toddler crawled all over him and tried to pull his right ear off.

'From 1986 until 1993 he was in jail.'

It was slightly odd because the war was long gone by 1993.

Hamid, however, was unconcerned about this discrepancy.

'This is Afghanistan. Once you go to prison it's hard to get out again.'

The story told to me was that Abdul Latiff had joined Ismail Khan's Jamiat-i-Islami group of mujahedeen during the war, but had left them because they didn't pay enough money. This highlighted one of the problems during the conflict which I had experienced at first hand, and that was not all of the fighters were full-time. In between battles there was work to be done, especially for the eldest sons in a family, and so it was often a case of work during the day and fight at night. In Abdul Latiff's case he had obviously not been as committed to the latter, and I wondered whether his lack of enthusiasm for Ismail Khan's cause might have kept him in the POW camp for longer than was necessary, especially when that particular individual assumed control of it and everything else at the end of the war.

Abdul Latiff had paid for his decision to abstain from fighting. He had been chucked in prison anyway by the Russians and then stayed there even after the war was over, possibly as a deserter.

Whatever the reason, I felt he deserved the good fortune that had landed him a job at the hotel and therefore, like Hamid, the chance of earning hard currency from cashed-up journalists.

The end of the evening was announced by a power failure. The hum of the generator was replaced by the woofing of dogs and it was decided that Abdul Latiff would drive us back to the hotel.

It was quite late and a tiredness had come over me that made the thought of bed extremely inviting. As I trudged up the stairs, stepping quietly past one of the young hotel workers who had rolled out a mat and gone to sleep on the landing, I imagined that I could hear someone whistling 'La Marseillaise', the national anthem of France. And so it was that the last thing on my mind as I dropped off to sleep was Aziz.

28

A good antidote to listlessness is to go and shoot a sub-machine-gun. Taking advantage of an offer from the hotel's proprietor the following day, I journeyed with him up into the hills that overlook Herat to a natural shooting gallery in a deep valley where we wouldn't be heard. On this occasion Hamid was unavailable, but it didn't matter because the proprietor spoke very slowly and rather simply for my benefit.

'Weather,' he said in Farsi, pointing up into a blue sky. 'Good!'

I replied also in Farsi, agreeing with him but adding that it was colder at night than when I first arrived, which probably meant winter was not far around the corner.

'Night!' he exclaimed. 'Cold,' and he shivered uncontrollably for good effect. It was clearly going to be an interesting day.

When we arrived he opened up the boot and lifted out the floor which hides the spare tyre. On this occasion there was no spare tyre, but a small arsenal of weaponry including two pistols, an AK47 and a large-calibre hunting rifle with a sniper scope attached, all wrapped in a blanket.

We left the car and walked over a low hill into a deep gulch. At one end was a sheer rocky cliff covered in bullet holes, so that the original rock face lay in fragments on the ground. Taking a piece of this rock he scratched a bull's-eye at about eye level and we retreated to a distance of approximately sixty or seventy metres.

First, out came the pistols which were Russian-made army issue. The problem was, from that distance it was difficult to know if anyone had actually hit the wall, let alone the target.

The AK47, however, was different. In my time before in Afghanistan I had only once carried a gun, and that was after having been shot at. It was a kind of madness that made me want to be able to shoot back, and I learned from Nebi how to disassemble, clean, assemble and fire my gun. But the madness lasted only a day and soon I was back to carrying a camera and learning how to keep my head down.

Now, the smell of that gun, of oil and iron, brought it all back. My hands seemed to find their own way over the surface, checking the safety and making sure there wasn't a bullet in the breech. I could even remember the combination of actions that would make the gun inoperable, until the reverse of those actions was carried out. But the one thing I couldn't get excited about was shooting at a rock wall. For some reason it simply wasn't for me. There was no skill involved; nothing could be easier than leaning forward and squeezing the trigger.

The hotel proprietor seemed to notice my reluctance and clearly felt that something larger was required. He offered the hunting rifle which I couldn't see the point of either. Then he gestured with a finger in the air as an idea occurred to him.

'Rocket!' he grinned. 'Good!'

With that he launched an invisible missile from an imaginary launcher on his shoulder. We watched it explode with devastating force against the wall at the end of the valley, leaving a hole the size of a man's head.

'No thanks,' I said.

'Tank!' he suggested.

'Better not. Tanks can be hard to hide in the boot of a car.'

I was something of a disappointment to him. But rather than suffering from a lack of testosterone, I was more preoccupied with the failure so far of my mission to find Nebi. It was unlikely he would be out in the countryside shooting guns, which made me question what I was doing there in the first place. Of course, it was a distraction that served to fill the day while I waited for that chance happening that would lead me to him; that million-to-one shot in the darkness.

The listlessness returned. It was an empty feeling, born of the growing realisation that perhaps this whole trip would be a 'so close, but yet so far' story, all bone and sinew without the meat of a happy ending.

Back outside the hotel, it took all of about five seconds to dispel the sense of creeping doubt.

'Mr Richard!' the voice called from above.

I looked up and met the gaze of one of the hotel cleaners leaning over a balcony and pointing urgently up a side street.

'Ghollum Sefarr is leaving. But he said he has news of your friend!'

'Where is he?' I shouted back against the noise of the street behind me. A particularly noisy bus driver was choosing this precise moment to blow his horn at some poor villager on a donkey. As a result, I could see lips moving but the sound they made was drowned out.

'Where? I couldn't hear you.'

'The airport! He is flying today to Kabul!'

'When did he leave?'

'An hour ago.'

This was serious. Ghollum Sefarr would not have left a message like this if he didn't have something important to say, and like many Afghans he would say it only to the recipient's face. This was either because of security or illiteracy, although in Ghollum Sefarr's case I couldn't decide which.

Now was not the time to worry about it. Now was the time to grab a taxi and make like the wind. Luckily a group of them regularly collected across the road and there was one waiting on the curbside. I ran hell for leather through the traffic and jumped in.

'*Hawapeima*!' I yelled.

'*Cheh*?' said the driver.

'*Hawapeima*,' I said again, this time sticking my arms out like an aeroplane and making a zooming sound. It worked, and we were off at a sharpish pace through the traffic.

When we got to the airport it wasn't hard to find Ghollum Sefarr. There were only a few people waiting for the flight and they all appeared to be standing at the entrance. He walked over when he saw me and we shook hands, although this time I was mindful of his injury.

'Goodbye my friend,' he said. 'I hope that I see you in the Panshir one day.'

'*Insha'allah*,' I said. 'They said you had news for me.'

'Yes. Your friend, his name was Mohandaspoor?'

'That's right.'

'One of my drivers remembered someone of that name who used to work on the trucks. He was a mechanic.'

A few more pieces of the puzzle fell into place.

'Did they say where?'

'Yes, you should try looking along the street that leads to the *musallah*. There are many workshops there, but they are a close community. If he is as good as my driver said he was, they will know him.'

'Thank you, Ghollum Sefarr,' I said.

'No problem,' he replied, making his way back to the group who were now picking up their possessions and going inside. 'Remember, come to the Panshir in the spring. We will hunt for ibex in the mountains.'

With that he was gone, but it was thanks to this man that I had a new lead to follow, and with that came a new strength. The taxi which had brought me was still waiting nearby and so I jumped back in, only to find the driver missing. Looking around I finally spotted him coming out from behind a low wall, still doing up his trousers.

'Would you get a move on!' I said in English.

'Cheh?' he replied.

I pointed back the way we had come and tapped my watch. He grumbled something as he slid behind the wheel that sounded very much like an insult.

Eventually we got back to the centre of the city and I paid him more than he was asking. Then I started walking towards the *musallah* whose majestic minarets were visible between the buildings. It wasn't far, but it was through a part of the city that was heavily congested and walking was a faster form of transport by far. Donkeys, mules and horse-drawn carts slowed down a motor vehicle's progress.

Along the way I passed myriads of fabric stalls selling materials of all colours of the rainbow, then shops selling pots of copper and steel, followed by the Afghan's version of the general store which sold everything from combs to cumin. In each store the owner sat, lord and master over his domain, sipping tea or chatting with a neighbour while the constant flow of people passed by.

After a time the roads widened and I found myself looking down a long, open street with the five remaining minarets belonging to the *musallah* standing at the far end. Already the mood had changed from the hectic bargaining of retailers to the banging of machinery and the thump of metal on metal. Every second business had some old truck or bus, usually standing on blocks, standing out in front like a beached whale.

I chose the first one and interrupted a man who was squatting on the ground washing an oil filter in a plastic tub of soapy water the colour of ink.

'*As'salaam aleikum,*' he said.

'*Aleikum salaam. Mahn donbal Nebi Mohandaspoor hastam.*'

Roughly translated it meant, 'Peace be upon you. I am looking for Nebi Mohandaspoor.'

But sometimes the sentence we know in English doesn't transfer well into colloquial Afghan. Especially right out of the blue without any of the other formal introductions. This might explain why the look I was now getting approached outright confusion.

I waved a hand and thought it better to start anew at the next workshop.

Once again I repeated the phrase, but not before wishing upon this next fellow a long life, without fatigue, and generally enquiring as to the health of his legs.

The reaction was an immediate improvement. He bestowed upon me an equal measure of good fortune without tiredness, as is the Afghan way. But in reply to my statement I met again a bemused look.

In a way it was completely justified. A stranger walks up to you and tells you in a big loud voice he is looking for this

148

person. You think, OK, but what has this got to do with me for pity's sake? Go away you loon!

Fortunately, I realised my mistake and was able to formulate a simple question rather than a declaration of intent. I asked him if he knew of Nebi, and this immediately extracted a more positive reply.

Actually it was a grunt. Not just an ordinary grunt, but a grunt with a hand signal. He pointed across the road to a small shop sandwiched in between a place selling steel doors and another trading in recently felled saplings which would one day be used for scaffolding.

I was met by a thin, elderly man with thick round glasses and two young boys in grease-stained clothes who stared up at me in wonder. I went through the usual greetings and started in on my request. The old man heard me out and then began jabbering back. Only he had no teeth which affected his speech and made it impossible to understand. By now a growing audience had gathered round and the resulting commotion made communication even harder. I was beginning to despair when a gruff voice in English came from inside the workshop.

'What do you want?'

I looked up. Coming out of the dark interior into the sunshine and rubbing his hands on a cloth was a man in western military clothes. He was not Afghani, his skin was too dark and his face more rounded, but I guessed he was probably from one of the Arab states.

'I'm looking for someone,' I said.

'Why?'

'Because . . .'

The Arab interrupted.

'This person owes you money?'

'No.'

'You have something to give him?'

'No, not really.'

'Who are you? Journalist? Doctor?'

'I'm neither. I'm just a traveller looking for a friend.'

The interrogation continued, for that was what it was, until all parties were satisfied that I wasn't after money or revenge or whatever else they suspected. The Arab translated for the crowd and he seemed to enjoy the power this gave him, although for the most part he was curt and abrupt with me. I asked him where he was from and he dismissed the question out of hand. It came as something of a surprise therefore when he indicated that I should accompany him on the back of a motorbike.

'Where to?'

'Back to your hotel.'

'Why?'

'Because the person you seek is not here. He has gone, but they will find him for you,' and he indicated with his arm to the group who surrounded us.

From inside the workshop he wheeled a Japanese trail-bike and with a kick of the starter the engine roared into life. The Arab got on and flicked his head to the seat behind him. I hesitated and he gunned the engine aggressively. Accepting a ride from this guy probably wasn't the safest option, but under the circumstances, declining would have possibly upset the delicate nature of my relationship with these people. It seemed I had made some kind of definite progress, but in exactly which direction I couldn't be sure. I climbed on the back of the bike and only just managed to hang on as the Arab took off in a cloud of dust. Within minutes, however, I was back at the hotel.

Hamid was sunning himself in a chair near the entrance.

'Did you find him?' he asked cheerily.

'Who?'

'Your friend.'

I thought about it for a moment before replying.

'Well, I think, yes. Maybe. Apparently, he is going to find me.'

Hamid drew up another chair beside him and patted the seat.

'In Afghanistan we have a saying. Patience is bitter, but its fruit is sweet.'

Later on there was a loud commotion in the street and a lot of shouting and waving of fists. Two men were having a go at each other over who was responsible for denting the other's car. It was getting nasty. One of the men went back to his vehicle and pulled out a gun. He fired a shot into the air and then proceeded to wave the weapon about over his head, screaming like a banshee.

Suddenly two soldiers appeared in green army uniforms and the sight of them calmed him down. He eventually put the gun away and both drivers got back into their cars and drove off, leaving the traffic to flow freely once more.

From our position in the sun, seated on our white plastic chairs, this strange incident was as if an amateur playgroup had put on a special matinée show for our viewing pleasure. We should have applauded perhaps, and then popped out for ice-creams. Instead, Hamid was impassive.

'Ramadan,' he muttered.

'Ramadan?'

'Today is the first day of Ramadan, the Muslim month of fasting. These things happen because everyone is hungry.'

The approach of this important religious date had totally passed me by. It explained a number of other things, most importantly the mood of the people I had run into that day. Except for Ghollum Sefarr, who was his usual cheery self (perhaps also because as a traveller he was exempt from the law), the taxi driver, the mechanics near the *musallah* and the Arab had all been a touch unfriendly. But then so would you if you had not eaten a meal since four in the morning, and the next one was not until after sunset.

'Will you fast?' I asked.

'Of course, but it is not necessary for you to make this sacrifice. Although if you do eat or drink during the day, it is best if you do it in your room,' he warned.

One of the many beggars who haunted the streets came up and Hamid was quick to pull out a wad of notes and peel off a few hundred rupiyeh for the man. It was something I saw him do on a daily basis, sometimes without even being asked. He would find beggars to give money to that I hadn't even noticed. The amounts he gave were not great, but that did not matter to the wretched upturned hands of those who relied upon his charity. After a while I started keeping a similar stash of notes in my top pocket. Not because I felt I should, but because I could.

After the beggar had gone, Hamid got up and dusted off his clothes.

'You must excuse me. Now I must go to the mosque to perform the prayer.'

He put his hands behind his ears, simulating the action performed by all Muslims at the start of prayer, to show they are listening to the words of Allah.

He went to go and then stopped.

'By the way,' he said. 'Yesterday in Seoshan, the people were talking about Osama bin Laden.'

'Yes.'

'It may interest you to know that he stayed here once at the Hotel Mowafaq.'

'You're joking!'

'No.'

'Not in my room I hope,' I said.

He laughed and his eyes sparkled with typical impishness.

'No, not in your room,' he replied.

'Glad to hear it.'

He started walking again and delivered the last line over his shoulder.

'It was the one next door.'

29

At dinner in the second-floor eating room, where the tables were all covered in white plastic mats printed with red roses, I was invited to join two Afghan men who had arrived that day from London. They had heard about the foreigner on the fourth floor and were keen to talk.

They were sitting near a window overlooking the lampless street. Nearby was a poster for 'Pine Super Slims' cigarettes. ENJOY THE TASTE OF AMERICA it said. There was also a picture of a pheasant in flight with the word PULL written in large letters below it.

'My name is Ghollum Mustafa and this is my cousin Sayyid.'

Ghollum Mustafa stood up politely as I sat down in the spare seat. He was a slightly built man with glasses that gave him the pronounced air of an academic. Sayyid, however, was tall and rangy looking, but said little. The reason was obvious. Ghollum Mustafa was not short on conversation.

'We have just come from the airport. What a journey! Madness! I am so tired I cannot think straight. What is there to eat here?'

I looked around at the other tables where men with bushy black beards and neatly wound turbans were tucking into a communal plate of rice and meat.

'I think the kitchen is all out of smoked salmon, and we finished the beluga yesterday, so it looks like donkey again.'

There was a slight delay before Ghollum Mustafa laughed.

Sayyid joined in too a heartbeat later.

'So tell me,' continued Ghollum Mustafa. 'Do you know if there are any flights to Kabul?'

'Three times a week, or so I'm told. One way US$150 for foreigners and US$50 for the locals.'

'Ah, unfortunately I have only a British passport these days. This is the first time in Afghanistan for nearly twenty-five years.'

Ghollum Mustafa hailed from Oxford while Sayyid had been living in Mashad for most of his life and had only recently joined his cousin in England. I learned that both were on something of an intellectual mission. Ghollum Mustafa had in his possession one of the largest collections of Afghan books which he had rescued from Kabul University before the Soviet invasion in 1979. Since then he had added to the collection until it crowded every wall space of his tiny flat, and that was the reason he had chosen this moment to return them.

'There are so many books, so many, many precious volumes that belong back in Kabul. Sometimes I cannot sleep because I worry about them. It is a great responsibility.'

The university were expecting his arrival in the next few days and once a proper place for their safekeeping was found, then the transfer could take place. His greatest fear was how to transport them from Oxford to Kabul. There were too many to airfreight because it would cost the earth. The idea he had come up with was to buy an old ambulance cheaply in Germany, take it back to Oxford, pack it full of the books and then drive all the way to Kabul.

'Why an ambulance?' I said.

'Because Afghanistan needs ambulances. It could be put to good use once I have delivered the books.'

I had to admit it was a good idea and I was able to tell him about the various borders he would have to cross along the way. Iran would be troublesome, given the government's nervousness about printed material from overseas, but not impossible. Then there would be the roads in Afghanistan to contend with, or the lack thereof. I also passed on Ghollum Sefarr's reports of robbers and thieves along the way and the blood drained from his face.

'This would be my worst nightmare,' he murmured.

'You could hire security?'

'Guns!'

He shuddered at the thought. Perhaps the idea of airfreight was beginning to sound more appealing. At least his books would not fall into the hands of some renegade who would take great joy in watching them burn.

'The Taliban have a lot to answer for,' he said grimly. 'You realise, of course, they are the product of American foreign policy?'

In 1979, when the Soviets invaded Afghanistan, President Jimmy Carter provided the mujahedeen with US\$30 million in covert aid through the Pakistani secret service, who supplied their own favoured rebel commanders, mainly Pashtuns with tribal connections across the border. Many of these commanders, like Gulbuddin Hekmatyar, knew that there would be a power vacuum once the Russians were gone and they waited patiently, storing brand-new US weapons in their original containers.

Under the Reagan administration, covert aid increased, as did the number of refugees who fled to the camps in Pakistan. By the late 1980s, the value of US military assistance was in the hundreds of millions and small-time commanders controlled massive arsenals with trained armies that ran an economy based on drugs and smuggling. Traditional tribal laws were soon forgotten and the dollar and the gun were the only things that mattered.

After February 1989 when the Soviets withdrew, civil war continued until mujahedeen forces moved in on cities like Herat and Kabul in 1992, ousting the Russian puppet President Najibullah. Guerrilla, religious and intellectual leaders quickly established a sort of Islamic republic, but it collapsed soon afterwards. There were simply too many people with too many guns for any voice of reason to be heard.

Meanwhile, in Quetta and Peshawar, large numbers of Afghan refugees were being educated in Islamic schools by hard-line mullahs who told the young men, or Talibs, to return to Afghanistan to drive out the armed warlords.

One 35-year-old mullah named Muhammad Omar began the uprising, and with the financial backing of a few Pakistani and Saudi businessmen (namely Osama bin Laden who donated several thousand black Toyota jeeps) they rose up from the south and took the regions one at a time, sweeping all before them with their brutal brand of justice, scaring the warlords into their mountain hideouts or into exile in Iran.

Afghanistan was on its way to becoming an emirate under Shahria law, a product of western intervention, not just America's, but from all sides.

Ghollum Mustafa was an educated man, a socio-anthropologist by trade who knew many of his country's most prominent thinkers courtesy of the lecture theatre and various speaking circles where he was a regular contributor. But neither he nor they resided in Afghanistan, apparently.

'Will you return here to live one day?'

'I would like to, but . . .'

He was looking round at his humble surroundings and I imagined him taking a white glove to the tabletops.

'It doesn't have to be this dirty. They could do something to clean this place. We are Muslims and being clean is part of our religion.'

I didn't have the heart to tell him that the Hotel Mowafaq had already been spruced up only a few years ago. It was one-star accommodation, but still probably one of the best hotels in the country. There were far worse places.

'You've been away too long,' I told him.

30

In contrast, my own time in Afghanistan was beginning to draw to a close. It happened one day when a trail-bike roared up to me as I was watching a football match from the side of the road. The field was a rock-hard clearing in a park dotted with pines and the players tackled each other upright, not prepared to risk anything like a sliding tackle. Some had boots, others wore bare feet and the goalie had on a Manchester United strip with the number 7 on his back.

Beckham mania stretched even this far.

The Arab was still in his military get-up but wore Saddam-style sunglasses making it difficult to see his eyes. His no-nonsense style of communication remained in evidence also.

'Get on,' he said, kicking the bike into gear so that it jumped forward a few inches.

'Sure is great to see you again,' I said, with a heavy hint of sarcasm. 'Thanks very much. Don't mind if I do.'

On the way, we passed a long-limbed man in rags who was standing in the road with his hands upraised to the sky. At regular intervals he was bringing them down hard on his head and wailing.

'Where are we going?' I asked.

Either my words were lost in the wind or he wasn't bothering to answer. He simply drove on, weaving in and out of the cars and trucks until we came to a halt outside a place where the money-lenders gathered with their huge wads of cash. There was quite a crowd of them, more than usual, and I could see that some were trading in the crisp, clean bills of the new Afghan currency.

Through an arched entranceway that led to a rear courtyard filled with dead plants we eventually came to a multi-level marketplace, not unlike the Serai Sayid in Mashad except this one was open to the elements. On all sides were terraces that looked down to the courtyard, and on these terraces were shops that traded in all manner of goods. Television sets fought for space with glass cases filled with pretty glass beads. Rolls of cloth stood vertically in rows, dark grey pinstripes on one side and bright red chiffon on the other. There were also shops that sold nothing but the sky-blue *burqas* every woman wore of their own accord.

The Arab took the steps two at a time to the second floor and we stopped outside a place that dealt in second-hand books. He slipped off his sandals and I followed suit, although it took me longer to get my boots off. As I was bent down untying laces I could hear him talking to someone within the store. That some-one, as I discovered shortly afterwards, was none other than Nasur Ahmad Najar, the ex-English teacher, the man I had first met upon walking into the Hezbollah offices in Mashad all those years ago. He had been their manager, someone who looked after the paperwork and administration, but he had also been the architect of my first journey into Afghanistan.

He was older and perhaps a little smaller even, but I would have recognised him anywhere.

'You haven't changed much,' he said.

'I was going to say that about you.'

He went to shake my hand but I couldn't resist hugging him, even though he was slightly uncomfortable. Out of the corner of my eye I could see the Arab at the doorway slipping on his sandals again. Once he had gone, Nasur Ahmad was a little more relaxed.

'Come, sit down and have some tea,' he smiled. 'I must fast but you do not need to.'

He went to the door and called out to someone down below. A younger voice could be heard in reply and fairly soon a small lad arrived with a single glass of the hot amber liquid.

I was full of questions. Who was the Arab, what was Nasur Ahmad's connection with the small mechanics' workshop near the *musallah* and most importantly, where was Nebi?

Nasur Ahmad grinned and leaned forwards.

'Firstly, if you want to know something in this town, you come to me. Everyone knows this. So when you spoke with those men near the *musallah* of Queen Gawhar Shad, naturally they told me about you. Then I spoke to Hamid after evening prayer and I realised who you were. Do you know, everyone at Hezbollah thinks you are dead?'

'Apparently so. I've already been to see Baba Khan and the others in Mashad. They thought they were looking at a ghost.'

He let out a chuckle.

'Secondly, the man who brought you here is trouble. He has problems, up here,' and he twirled a finger near the side of his head. 'Too much hate in one man is bad, and I am a little surprised he offered to help you. Perhaps there is hope for him yet. Finally, I can tell you where Nebi is, although you have a long journey ahead of you to reach him. Nebi is in Mashad.'

Nasur Ahmad filled in the blanks. He described how Nebi had indeed worked as a mechanic, but that he had returned to Mashad for the sake of his family. The schools in Herat were not good, life was hard and he had wanted something better for them and his wife.

'You remember Karim?'

Karim Esmailzadeh had been the young warrior poet who had travelled with Nebi and me on several occasions.

'Well, Nebi is married to Karim's sister,' he said.

'And they all live in Mashad?'

'Yes, since four months ago. But it would be very difficult for you to find them. They are not legally allowed to be in Iran, and so they are hiding.'

'But you know where they live?'

'I will write it down for you.'

Nasur Ahmad scribbled a few lines in English into my journal, and then repeated the address in Farsi underneath. After all this time, and all the doubt and worry, I was suddenly in possession of the one item that would make all of it worthwhile.

'Now I want you to give me something in return.'

'What?'

'Your story. What happened after you left Herat? Where do you live. Your work? Everything.'

For the rest of the day I was able to return the favour. Nasur Ahmad made me leave nothing out. If there was even a hint of skipping something he would complain bitterly. For my own sake I was anxious to know the same about him, but I had to wait until he was satisfied that every part was told.

Finally, the subject turned to him and his life in the years since we last met. It was a humbling story. Our two lives could not have been more different. While I had spoken of good times and achievements, his was a story of hardship and despair. After the war he had tried to teach again, his eyes lighting up again as he remembered those days, but it was a fleeting glimmer. Again the Taliban had served only to wreck his life, arriving at the school one morning to take away the books that smacked of the minority Shia version of Islam and magazines that showed pictures of humans and animals – sacrilegious in the Taliban's eyes.

One year, the Taliban governor of Herat, a Pashtun by the name of Abdulman Jahedwal, came to Herat's public library with a retinue of armed guards and took away about half its collection.

I looked around his small shop at the shelves that groaned under the weight of literature.

'But they didn't get everything,' he said.

From over the rooftops came the call to prayer, the sound of which stirred a flock of pigeons somewhere above us. The flapping of their wings echoed loudly within the building.

'You must come again, when we have more time.'

'You will be here?' I asked.

'This is my home,' he replied matter-of-factly.

It was then I noticed the fold-up bed in the corner and the small gas stove beside it.

31

Hamid was the first person I saw the next morning. It was 4 a.m. and I was hungry for breakfast. He was carrying a candle out to the generator hut so that he could see to start the engine. I followed him through the back door past the large square hole in the ground that was ever so faintly blue in colour. It was an empty swimming pool. The dark shape at one end was a diving board.

'I should come back in the summer,' I said after a while. 'And bring my togs.'

'Togs? What are togs?' he said as the big diesel coughed a smoker's cough and chugged into life.

'Bathing shorts. Swimming trunks. Board shorts.'

'Ah yes,' he remembered. 'You live near the ocean.'

It brought back the subject of his sister and the letter we had sent to Aziz, of whom there was still no news. Time was running out for her, he said. The doctors had done all they could and were hinting that the problem was not physical but possibly mental. The changes in personality, the mood swings from quiet to hysterical were being blamed on a psychological condition that should be treated in Pakistan, or as a last resort, Kabul.

'Perhaps in a few days we will have to move her,' he admitted.

The mention of Kabul's supposed psychiatric facilities brought back the terrible images from a documentary I had seen only last year – people chained to walls and kept in tiny, windowless rooms that were washed out with a bucket of water each day to clear away the excrement. Life could not get any worse.

We sat in silence over breakfast until Hamid, judging the moment, turned to me and asked quietly, 'When do you go?'

'Tomorrow, or the day after.'

'There are cars and vans going to the border each morning about this time. I can arrange it for you if you wish.'

'That would be fine.'

'The day after tomorrow?'

'Sure. The day after tomorrow.'

The last couple of days were spent visiting those places that had caused so many writers and travellers throughout the centuries to fall in love with Herat. Even the 16th-century Moghul emperor Babur, writing in his memoirs, said 'the whole habitable world had not such a town as Herat', which was a tribute to a time when the western Afghan city was celebrated as a centre for the sciences and arts.

We went to Gazargah, the peaceful shrine of the 11th-century Sufi poet and philosopher Khwaja Abdulla Ansari, which was situated up in the hills overlooking the city. An ancient pistachio tree had grown straight out of the tomb and was almost as revered amongst the faithful as the shrine itself. Lines of beggars and their beggar children preyed upon us and the small stash of notes I carried was long gone before I made it back to the car.

It felt like I was someone who was packing up a house so that it could be closed for an indefinite period, giving away the things that had been hoarded away and were now of no importance.

At the old citadel near the hotel, we tried to gain access but were denied permission. Built by Alexander the Great, this imposing fortress had been held by the Ghaznavids, the Seljuks, the Ghorids, the Mongols, the Timurids, the Safavids and was now in the hands of a superior official who gazed at my partially concealed camera with open contempt.

I did make sure to visit Nasur Ahmad Najar again, but we had said perhaps all that had to be said, and now there was nothing more. I bade him farewell and wished him good fortune. He made me promise to remember him to my family.

In the end, I still had some unfinished business over the

border in Mashad and my focus was starting to turn away from Afghanistan and back to Iran. When the morning for my departure came, with a black ex-Taliban Toyota Hilux waiting out in the street in the pre-dawn light, I knew it was time. There were no great farewells, just a sleepy-eyed Hamid who wrote down my home address and pledged to let me know if Aziz ever did show up.

Then I was sandwiched into the back seat beside a one-eyed man and his wife, whose stomach wriggled and jiggled because of the baby she cradled under her *burqa* of cornflower blue.

It was more comfortable than the bus, and a great deal faster, and by midday I was walking from the dusty track of Afghanistan onto the grey ribbon of tarmac that stretched across no-man's-land and into Iran.

32

The next morning began clear and bright as the sun rose over the golden dome of Imam Reza's shrine, casting long shadows across the pilgrims who, having completed their first act of devotion for the day, were probably thinking more about breakfast.

I washed in the sink in my room at the Qods Hotel and reluctantly combed the last dusty remnants of Afghanistan out of my beard, thinking all the while about the day before.

Somewhere on the road between the border and Mashad, I decided I had hitched a ride with the craziest man alive when for the hundredth time he threw back his head, laughed in a manner that suggested the entire machine plant was unhinged rather than just a screw being loose, and all for no apparent reason.

His name was Jigger, or at least that was the word he had repeated over and over with extreme hilarity whenever he referred to himself. Later I discovered Jigger means 'lover' in Farsi, which was as weird as the man himself. I'm not saying he was ugly, but he was certainly no Clark Gable.

What's more, everyone on the road had known him. Cars that were headed in the opposite direction flashed their lights at us which ignited a fresh bout of madness. Even when we had pulled in for petrol, the owner seemed to know what to expect and had gone out of his way to push the right buttons to activate Jigger's lunatic inclinations.

For the first half an hour it had been funny. By the time the second thirty minutes was up the joke was starting to wear a little thin. Another hour on and still with Mashad nowhere in sight, I had seriously entertained the idea of jumping from his fast-moving vehicle.

What saved me was a near head-on collision with a speeding goods truck. Jigger had failed to see it coming over the brow of a hill, and because he drove in the middle of the road most of the time, it was an extremely close call. I had shouted, he had swerved, and ten tonnes of metal and rubber flashed by. After that incident, the rest of the journey had passed in a more sober mood.

Because of Ramadan, breakfast was a handful of raisins and dried apricots, plus some of yesterday's bread from the Mowafaq Hotel. Then I set out for Hezbollah with the journal containing Nebi's address safely tucked away in my shoulder-bag. Rather than simply turn up on his doorstep unannounced, I reasoned it might be better to involve Baba Khan to see if he could make contact first. If what Nasur Ahmad Najar had said was true about Nebi's illegal status and therefore caginess, discretion might prove the better part of valour.

But at Hezbollah there was something wrong. The usually cheery reception was muted and dull, and I was concerned that I had done something to offend one of them. As it turned out, it was not me but the Iranian government. The day before two officials had arrived from Tehran with instructions to begin closing down the office. Iran no longer needed to support the Afghan Hezbollah in Mashad. They wanted the Afghans to return to their own country, which included Baba Khan and the others.

I found them in one of the upstairs rooms, twiddling their prayer beads and looking despondently at the ground.

'Where have you been?' said a man called Sardegh.

'Herat.'

Eyes immediately raised themselves from the floor and turned away from gazing out of the window.

'Speak. Tell us, how does it look to you?' piped up a man known only as Garbeh. He was slightly built but a fast and nimble fighter of great renown.

'They are painting the seats in the park.'

It wasn't much but it was all I could think of at the time. However, this seemed to meet with general approval.

'Ismail Khan has signed a deal with Turkmenistan to provide electricity.'

Again heads nodded, but ironically not with as much enthusiasm.

'And I have found Nebi,' I announced.

This last piece of news was of far greater interest. I showed them the page in my journal and it was handed round the room. Fingers followed the lines of Persian script from right to left and then jabbed at the paper when a landmark was recognised. In this part of the world addresses start with numbers and streets, but because in Iran, especially, so many streets had their names changed after the Revolution, people started adding descriptions like 'on the right side of the road, near the three large grain silos'.

And so it was with Nebi.

Baba Khan knew the location well and immediately despatched a runner, one of the younger men who raced around on small 100-cc motorbikes, to go there and bring him back.

We waited.

Tea was brought for me alone.

The others drifted in and out haphazardly and I was aware of the sun creeping across the carpeted floor. Ali the wrestler came in and jokingly offered to fight me to help pass the time.

Then came the noise of a motorbike outside the window, followed soon after by a solitary pair of footsteps coming slowly up the stone stairs. They paused outside the curtain that hung across the door, shoes were slipped off and left neatly to one side, then with a dramatic flick the curtain parted and there he stood.

Time slows down at these moments. Hearing closes down and speech is made redundant. It appears to take an age for anything to happen as the eyes move quickly to tell the story, revealing details that might normally be missed. You see calloused hands and patched brown trousers, a white shirt pocket with a blue pen, a button missing, hair brushed, face clean-shaven and broad which hints at the faint trace of Mongol ancestry, a smile wide and sure, and then the eyes – eyes that are dark like a hawk's, looking straight back at you.

But time can be slowed for only a while. Then it must catch up to the present again. So it accelerates forward rapidly – one minute you are sitting and the next you are standing, embracing, slapping and being slapped on the back, kissing and being kissed on either cheek. Finally, hearing and speech return in an instant, flooding the room with exclamations of joy and shouts of incredulity, the perfectly wonderful sound of old friends greeting.

'I thought you . . .' he said without finishing.

'Yes, I know. Dead.'

He called me Massoud, the name he gave me, and then stopped.

'What is your real name?'

'Richard.'

'Mister Richard,' he corrected.

I told him, 'Just Richard is better,' but he refused.

Stepping back I could see the grey hair around the temples and the few extra lines on his face, but he was still fit and strong. Years of manual labour had seen to that. He took a seat by the window and the strong sunlight coming in over his shoulder produced a halo effect round his upper body.

'How are you?' I asked.

'Good, Mister Richard.'

'And you have a wife and children now.'

'Three boys and a girl.'

'I have only two. A boy and a girl.'

'Praise be to God. And a woman?'

I smiled.

'Yes, of course,' I said. 'First the woman and then the children.'

The entire room erupted with laughter and Ali slapped me hard on the shoulder. It was just like the old times, and for much of the time we went back over those days to discover things we had forgotten or not known. I for one was saddened to learn that a man I had come to respect greatly, Haji Wahab, was one of those killed in the fighting that followed my departure from Herat. He had been gunned down while riding a motorbike near the village of Korskack, leaving a wife and children whom I had met. Soon after, Nebi himself suffered the injuries that would end his part in the war.

Of my experiences in crossing the country Nebi was naturally curious. There was much to fill in, too much for one sitting in fact, and before long he stood up to go.

'Mister Richard. Harrakat,' he said, pointing to the door.

'Where?'

'Your hotel. We will pick up your bags and then you can come to stay in my house.'

It was an offer I was not about to refuse, but as it happened there was an even greater reason for me to go with him. My arrival on this particular day was hugely significant. That night his brother was to be married and a big party was planned. I was to be a late entry, as a guest of honour, at an Afghan wedding.

Like so many others, Nebi rode without a helmet on a 100-cc Taztac motorbike. Only he had taken its insignia off and replaced it with a Honda badge.

Weaving in and out of the traffic, we collected my things from the hotel and then took an off-ramp from the new circular expressway under the shrine to get to his home. It was near a cluster of towering grain silos, in a quiet, leafy suburb where children played soccer in the street and few cars troubled their game.

His house, like all the others, was behind an iron door set into a wall which led through to a courtyard with a pond at its centre. I looked for signs of life but there were none. A grapevine still carrying some of its fruit stretched over a wooden trellis connecting the house to a washroom and toilet.

Leaving our shoes at the door, I was shown into a two-roomed home with doors between the rooms that could be closed for privacy, plus a kitchen which was curtained off. It was through this that Nebi's wife appeared moments later, wearing a black chador and a pretty smile. Instead of her gaze being glued to the floor, as I had so often witnessed in Iran, she looked at me confidently and then somewhat curiously as Nebi explained who I was.

'I know your brother, Karim,' I said.

At this she positively beamed and invited me to sit down on the floor where there were long pillows against the wall to lean against. Then she went back to the kitchen to make tea.

'Mister Richard,' said Nebi. 'Karim is in Kabul.'

'Has he been there long?'

Nebi called through to the kitchen and his wife's reply bounced back through the curtain.

'Six months,' he said. 'But he returns in one month. How long can you stay?'

'Not that long, I am sorry.'

It brought back the issue of my visa which had come from the Embassy in Herat. It was a seven-day transit visa, already a day old. I showed it to him and then remembered Nebi couldn't read. He flicked through the pages of the passport and stopped only when it came to the photograph. When his wife returned and sat beside him, it was she who found the visa and read it out loud.

He shook his head, but then smiled.

'But you are alive! Massoud is alive!'

That day I learned how Nebi had been one of the lucky ones to survive the mine and of his time in hospital, of his family's return to Herat and the subsequent disillusionment with that city. He had spent so long fighting for its freedom, that when freedom came it wasn't enough. Now he had a business making wooden entertainment centres which many homes required to house their television sets and video-disc players. He had one of these in the corner of the room. It was made from particle board and painted over in dark grey that matched the colour of his TV and VCD player.

There were a number of movies standing side by side on a shelf in their plastic cases, all of which were pirated copies from

Pakistan. The shops in Iran were full of these, mostly action and horror films, some not even released yet in the cinemas at home. I looked at the cover of a film called *Eight-legged Freaks*, which showed David Arquette running from a horde of huge mutant spiders. Underneath in scary type it read: *Let the squashing begin!*

Just then a commotion at the door erupted in a fury of excitement. Nebi's children raced in carrying schoolbags but stopped when they saw the stranger. I was introduced, one at a time, from the eldest to the youngest, to his only daughter Ghitee, and his sons Mahdi, Mohammad and last of all, little Massoud.

They were charming children, but I immediately felt a bond with the youngest, partly because we shared the same Afghan name.

The time for the celebrations to begin was soon upon us. Nebi's wife went to her sister's to get ready and from there she would join the other women in their own private ceremony. The men would have a separate get-together which, in true Afghan fashion Nebi warned me, would be a wild night.

It was, if anything, a massive understatement.

The evening began calmly enough in a large reception room with mirrors on the walls and ceiling, where roughly two hundred men were seated at tables piled high with sweet foods and fruit. Waiters in smart uniforms hustled and bustled, supplying endless amounts of tea to the guests, the majority of whom were dressed in western-style suits.

I was only mildly disappointed. I had expected flowing beards and turbans, curved knives stuck in leather belts and bandoliers across each shoulder. But it appeared the Afghans had adopted Iranian clothes, perhaps to blend in and not attract unwanted attention. 'When in Rome,' they say.

I sat next to a young man in a shiny black suit who was on the bride's side of the family and lived in Denmark. He spoke German to me in a high-pitched voice.

'*Ich bin ein salesman. Mit Bitburger Pils.*'

'Oh,' I replied, thinking an Afghan kid selling German beer to the Danes should be quite interesting. But it wasn't, and I couldn't get past the shiny suit and squeaky voice.

On my other side, however, was by his own admission a

world-famous tabla player by the name of Mohammad Saleem Khoshnawaz. The tabla is a kind of drum that originated in Northern India and had spread throughout the region. I asked him how he had learnt to play and the venerable Mohammad Saleem stroked his beard and gave me an old-fashioned look.

'I learned the tabla from my father, who learned from his father, who learned from his father.'

Later, I discovered that he was indeed famous and had performed in Turkey, Germany and the United States.

Within seconds the mood of the party swung from one end of the spectrum to the other. Suddenly, men who were up until now engaged in quiet conversation, were on their feet hooting and hollering. The groom had arrived and was making the rounds of his guests, greeting as many as possible. Before long he was being swept along by a tide of well-wishers who eventually dragged him down into a downstairs kitchen. I was part of the select group who witnessed the blessing of the food by Nebi's uncle, Ghollum Zabi, a man of boundless energy and the charismatic ability to command the attention of any audience, before we were again sucked upstairs on a wave of macho shouting and pushing.

Midnight approached as the pack feasted again, and when we were finished, appetites satiated and thirsts quenched, that was when the real fun began.

Two hundred or so men, by now in jubilant form, crowded into about seventy or eighty battered old Paykans to race the newly-weds (the bride in white lace having appeared from upstairs) seven times around the shrine of Imam Reza.

And what a race it was! The Mashad 500!

At speeds approaching one hundred kilometres an hour, which is top speed in a Paykan, the entire entourage took off up both sides of the road and ran after the lead car containing Mr and Mrs Mohandaspoor, heeding no traffic light nor keeping to any lane. As a result there were two crashes within the first five minutes and in each case fights broke out, causing everyone to pour out of the cars to help call it off. Then it was back into the car to continue, only to come to a skidding halt further up the road to pull apart another two or three who were slogging it out with each other.

When we finally came to the shrine it was a demolition derby as our wedding party ran into another similarly revved-up wedding party, and then ultimately a third, each performing the same mad chase. Countless broken tail-lights, dented bumpers and bruised egos later, we shot out at speed for the groom's house where a large tent had been erected in the front courtyard.

I finally caught up with a breathless Nebi outside.

'What was that?' I said incredulously.

'Afghans!' he said, shaking his head and laughing at the madness. '*Diwanyeh*!'

Inside, thick Persian and Afghan carpets were laid across the floor of the tent and someone had attached coloured streamers to the central pole. Men were already seated around the perimeter and others stood outside checking their cars. But when the band started playing an upbeat Bhangra-style number, everyone crowded inside and leapt to their feet to dance. There were no women, and not a drop of alcohol, but it was an incredible display of exuberance from an all-male group.

Most danced like strutting, handsome peacocks, but others took on a different role. Their hands twisted and twirled at the wrist in mock simulation of the sultry *houri* of a Sultan's palace. Eyes fluttered and bottoms wriggled and jerked to the beat. And not just the men; their sons took the part of hip-swaying Fatimas, the best of whom had money stuffed into their mouths to roars of delight from the crowd.

On and on it went through the night, the music ranging from heart-pumping, foot-tapping songs of love and battle, to gentle ballads where the tabla player proved his mastery by weaving intricate beats and rhythms together in a way that swept us all along.

At one stage the groom made an appearance, slightly red-cheeked and obviously fresh from the matrimonial bed, to join his friends and family in this dance of men.

When it was over, there was nothing left to give, nothing left to say, nothing left to add. The exhaustion came from the exertion of dancing, but also from the energy-sapping nature of the experience. It was life led at the very edge.

In the end, we walked outside to witness the dawn light chasing the stars from the East, like a real-life version of the *Rubaiyat* of Omar Khayyam.

33

There were five of us on his little motorbike. Massoud on the petrol tank, Nebi steering, then me, followed by Mohammad with Mahdi perched at the rear. We were like one of those circus acts when all the clowns climb aboard a mini-scooter and race about the ring, hanging from every side.

Our destination that afternoon was an amusement park situated a few kilometres outside the city gates, although every-one else in Mashad seemed to have the same idea. The main intersections were chaotic because no one heeded the traffic lights nor the white-gloved traffic policemen who waved furiously at everyone from the safety of their colourfully painted platforms. Fortunately, motorbikes – even ones as loaded down as ours – enjoyed a greater freedom than the Paykans that crawled along through the traffic. We rode smoothly through the gaps, crossed the centre line at regular intervals and mounted pavements to send pedestrians scattering. In this way, the entrance was soon reached.

Instead of going through the gates, however, Nebi took a side road and parked the bike well out of sight. As an illegal alien, he could not gain the necessary licences to be on the road and therefore was compelled to take precautions against being caught by any vigilant police officers.

We walked back to the main gates and wandered in. There was no ticket booth; entrance was free. The boys bought a packet of seeds to eat and ran off towards a massive rocky outcrop that had been turned into an adventure playground of tunnels and secret hideaways. Nebi and I strolled towards an overhead miniature railway line mounted on tall poles, in which young Mashadies were enjoying themselves. The teenage boys in one carriage were trying to catch up to the teenage girls in another, but they had become stuck on the track. The next carriage had a family of four on board and they were bumping into the boys from behind to try and get them going.

'Do you have this in your country?' asked Nebi.

'It's like this,' I replied, 'but different.'

Nebi smiled, showing off a set of clean white teeth. Then he pointed to a group of mullahs a short way off.

'Mr Richard, look. Do you have these?'

'No,' I said.

'Then I like your country. Very much.'

The mullahs were all in brown robes with black garments underneath and white turbans on their shaven heads. All wore glasses also, which I took to be a result of reading the *Koran* all day in the dimly lit confines of their mosques. Now, however, their eyes were gazing reproachfully at the adolescent antics above their heads.

Happily they didn't interfere, but this was probably because the girls were now a long way ahead of the boys.

We found a seat near a fountain and sat down to talk. A group of children ran past with red and yellow balloons that carried the unmistakable image of Mickey Mouse in silhouette.

'You and Hezbollah,' I said. 'Still friends?'

The shrug of his shoulders implied that he and they were not as close as had once been the case. There was a distance between them that had grown over time, he said. Hezbollah had been a second family to him, and to the others who fought amongst its ranks, but with the fighting over and the enemy sent packing, the fighters had been replaced with politicians vying for power.

'Haji Qarry Ahmad Ali is always in Tehran,' he pointed out. 'They want him to go against Ismail Khan in Herat.'

'And will he?'

'Haji Qarry is a clever man and Ismail Khan has a large army. Many tanks, many cars, many guns.'

I asked him if he still had the weapons he carried during the Soviet war.

'In the ground,' was his slightly sheepish reply. 'In the garden of my house in Herat.'

He paused for a few seconds, thought, and then continued, 'I also have an RPG in the roof of the toilet.'

It certainly painted an amusing picture. A rocket propelled grenade in the loo was, I felt, something that would take a while to find favour in the western world. Nevertheless, caught with your trousers down by some armed burglar, it might prove a highly effective way of asking them to leave.

Nebi's home in Herat turned out to be near the *musallah* which, of course, was quite close to my hotel. It was rented out to members of his wife's family at a measly rate, although his real-estate hopes for the future were great. One day it would be worth some money, situated so close to the city centre, and he would then sell it and build again someplace else.

'Or I will travel, like you,' he grinned. 'I would like to see your country where there are no mullahs. Maybe drink some whisky.'

'You drink whisky?'

'Just a little, Mister Richard,' and he brought his thumb and forefinger together so they almost touched.

A little later, once the boys had returned, we wandered off and found a *chai salonu* that was closed because of Ramadan and a man surreptitiously selling ice-cream out of an ice box on the back of his bike. It was strange to stand there and watch Nebi haggle with the man over the price of the cones. This was the Nebi who had fought in a war for more than half his life, who had almost certainly killed others in the course of defending his country, who knew how to lay mines and defuse them, fire mortars and fix captured machinery, and who had a small arsenal of destruction in the bathroom as well as buried in his back garden. Now he was a family man like me, buying special treats at the fair for his children and balking at the price.

This proved to be too much and the children, like all children, were miserable afterwards. I would have offered to pay but I knew it would have been an insult for me to do so.

Besides, the mullahs were a problem and Nebi I knew did not want trouble.

It was on the way back to the motorbike when we encountered the police. They were on the road outside the gates, stopping vehicles and checking licences at random. Nebi saw them at the same time as I did, but his reaction was quite different. He froze for a split second and then turned fully around, pretending to look at a bird on a wire and getting the boys to do the same, but all the while thinking of what to do next. A short while later we started off in another direction, away from the police, back towards the safety and anonymity of the fair-going crowds until the danger had passed. It was a brief but telling glimpse into the realities of his life as an illegal person in Iran.

That night was spent with Nebi's family, which included his sister-in-law and uncle, whom I had watched entertain everyone with his rousing and flamboyant behaviour at the wedding. Ghollum Zabi had worked with a number of relief organisations in Afghanistan and spoke halting English, which improved as the night wore on. Now he was unemployed and with a large family to feed.

'It is a pity,' he said, 'that we did not meet earlier. I would like to have been your translator in Afghanistan. I need money to send my wife to see her parents in Herat, money for visa also so that she can return to Iran.'

The amount he needed was thirty US dollars, a reasonably substantial amount for anyone in this part of the world, let alone an Afghan with no work in Mashad.

I suggested he be my translator for the night.

'Of course, but this I do for free. You are Nebi's friend and a guest in his home.'

The night was lively, as all occasions were it seemed when Ghollum Zabi was around. Nebi and his wife were able to ask many questions of me, through his uncle, that I would have found difficult to understand in Farsi. Questions relating to my work, my family, the children and of course, my book *Blue is the Colour of Heaven*, which described many of our shared experiences in Afghanistan. Nebi had already seen the photographs (torn from one of the damaged copies rescued from the Penguin book bin), one of which was of him as a younger man, but I had left the book itself behind in case an over-zealous border official decided it was somehow scandalous or anti-Islamic. Neither of which was the case, but I had erred on the side of caution nonetheless, not wanting to become another Salman Rushdie.

Far and away the most inquisitive person was the sister-in-law. She sat in the corner with a scarf over her head and across her mouth, firing questions at Ghollum Zabi so that I wasn't always sure who had asked them. They were intelligent, sometimes provocative queries about my opinions on Islam and Islamic culture. When she eventually broached the subject of women, it was the uncompromising tone in her voice that took me by surprise.

My answer had been on the flippant side. I had replied that I didn't see the point of a woman hiding her hair. It didn't make sense to me, or to anyone else from a western culture.

Hardly moving, her response was immediate, like a planned attack.

'You think Christianity does not embrace propriety?'

'Well, yes, but it doesn't make women cover themselves up,' I said.

'Then what about your Mary?'

I guessed she meant the mother of Jesus.

'What about her?' I said.

'She wore a scarf to cover her hair.'

That was a hard point to refute, since a collection of images came to mind at that moment of Mary dressed just like this. Even in the school plays I had been to, which occasionally contained some religious instruction thinly disguised as entertainment, the girls wore something over their heads – even if it was only an old tea-towel or a lace cloth from the hall table.

Before I had time to answer she was off again.

'And your nuns also.'

I was doing a lot of thinking at this point and not a lot of constructive argument. Yes, two thousand years ago in Palestine all women hid their hair and even today some Catholic nuns wore a habit that covered just about everything. But I pointed out, with perhaps more conviction than my line of reasoning deserved, the head-dress in Mary's time was probably an entirely practical way of keeping the dust out, shampoo being a distant invention, and in the nuns' case they were a small minority who were staunchly adhering to a way of life that had lost its relevance – not unlike Beefeaters at the Tower of London and some of the even more pompous costumes worn by members of the House of Lords.

When I'd said my piece Ghollum Zabi sat looking at me with a bemused expression. Then he turned to the woman in the corner and said, 'He doesn't know.'

I had to laugh.

Either it was because he was bored with the conversation or just simply tired of translating, he changed the subject onto something more to his liking.

'One day I want to own a Charlie,' he said.

'A Charlie? You want your own Prince of Wales?'

'Prince of whales?' he asked, obviously baffled. 'Whales I do not need, but a Charlie Davidson is what I dream of.'

'You mean Harley-Davidson.'

He looked up at the ceiling for a moment and then jerked a finger in the air.

'Yes, sorry. Thank you, you are right. It is Harley. The Fat Boy!' he exclaimed. 'I ride the Fat Boy through Mashad and get the girls to kiss old Zabi.'

He thought this was hilarious and translated his dream for the others to enjoy. It didn't go down well with Nebi's sister-in-law who remained unmoved in the corner, but everyone else was highly amused. From his position on the floor, he tore through the streets and most of the people in the room swayed their bodies in synch with his movements.

Finally, he gunned the engine once or twice, put the dream in neutral, then let the throaty burble of his imaginary motorbike splutter out.

'What is your dream?' he asked suddenly, lying down full length on the carpet and stretching out.

'It *was*,' I said, 'to find this man over here.'

I nodded to where Nebi was leaning against the opposite wall, silently watching me and listening. Nebi did not talk unless he had something to say, a characteristic I admired greatly, but on this occasion he could not have got a word in anyway.

'You have found your dream!' Ghollum Zabi roared, sitting upright again and holding his hands out, clutching at a pair of invisible handlebars.

'This is good. It means there is still hope yet for mine!'

34

The next morning, having slept fitfully thanks to the howling of wild cats, the hardness of the floor and because Nebi ground his teeth all through the night, I discovered him up, dressed and examining my small digital movie camera very closely. He was very inquisitive and wanted to know how to turn it on, how it worked, everything. I showed him these things, and how the LCD display swivelled round to face the front so that he could see himself on the screen. He recorded me sitting with his children over a breakfast of fried egg and bread. They were very excited, not just because of the camera, but because the eggs were a special treat.

When he was finished he turned it off, put it back near my bag where he had found it and joined us at the metre-square plastic mat on the floor that was our dining table.

'Mister Richard,' he said, scraping some egg off our shared plate with a folded piece of bread. 'Why did you really come back?'

The question caught me by surprise.

'I wanted to know what happened to you, and the others as well.'

He sat cross-legged, shoulders hunched over, chewing the food in his mouth. When he had finished he wiped his chin and chuckled. 'You were always curious. In Herat, some people thought you were a spy because you asked so many questions.'

'Really!'

'One man even wanted to sell you to the enemy.'

'A man from Hezbollah?' I asked.

'No, from Jamiat-i-Islami. You and I stayed one night in their *komiteh*. But only one night. In the morning . . .'

He smiled as he ran two fingers through the air before my eyes.

It was a long time ago, but I could faintly recall a hasty departure from one such place. The welcome had not been as warm on that occasion, and the faces that had stared back at me were blank and unresponsive, the kind that ask questions later.

It was a clear reminder of the debt I owed Nebi, a debt I would always struggle to repay. My return went some way to making good the outstanding account between us. But the fact was, it was a small repayment, and the interest was long overdue.

'I am sorry it has taken me so long,' I apologised. 'And I am also sorry that soon I will have to leave again.'

'You will be back, God willing. Afghanistan is your home now. This is your house. And the next time you must bring your family. Your children will play with my children and they can learn from each other.'

'What would they learn?' I asked.

After a moment's thought, he replied.

'Our songs.'

With that, Mohammad started to croon an Afghan love song in his native language of Dari, waving his head from side to side and stretching his arms out so that his hands could swirl and dance at the wrist. Laughing, Massoud and Mahdi joined in and soon their mother had poked her head around the corner to listen. She smiled so sweetly and proudly at the sight of her boys, it made me feel part of an extremely close group. Maybe it was just because of what Nebi had said moments before, but in a funny way, it did feel like being home again.

The song, I later discovered, was a tale of two fatherless brothers, the younger of whom left the home in the countryside to find work in the city, while the older remained behind to tend the fields and care for his family, as was expected of him. Many years passed and no word was heard from the younger sibling, until one day a magical white dove appeared in a tree with the sad news that he was lost in a valley far away and had become weak and close to death. The older brother could not leave the farm, so he asked the dove to carry a seedling from the fields he had worked in that day, to give to his ailing brother. This the dove agreed to do, and with that token of life, which was born in the soil and connected them together, the younger man was healed and made strong again.

It was a story that was simple enough, and possibly buried in ancient folklore I knew nothing about, but one whose basic narrative bore a striking resemblance to our own. Had I made a home in Afghanistan all those years ago, and then left to suffer a similar fate as in the song? Was Nebi the proof that all of it existed, that there was a base for a part of me to return to and be strengthened?

I asked Nebi, 'Does the brother return home again?'

'No, never,' he said.

'But why?' I protested.

He shrugged in his reply, as someone does when stating the obvious.

'Because he must find his own way.'

35

The day was spent in earnest at Nebi's workshop (a room no more than six metres by four with an iron door and a single window for light and ventilation in the roof), which was in a densely populated industrial area of Mashad, because a buyer had come in and placed an order that had to be completed quickly. Word of Nebi's invention, the entertainment console, had spread and this man was acting as a kind of retailer who would, it seemed, by his confident disposition, see to it that every home in the surrounding area had one.

While Nebi put together the pieces of wood, I stood in a makeshift spray booth outside in the street and applied the first coat of paint. One layer of white primer, after which would be added the undercoat, then three layers of gunship-grey enamel.

When we had completed as many as could be hung to dry in the limited space of his workshop, we went next door to the local barber to rest and admire his collection of bottled snakes.

There were four of them standing in a line on a shelf beside the mirror. Each jar was filled with a preservative liquid and out from this coloured gloom the coiled remains of four venomous reptiles were peering. Their unseeing eyes stared through the glass and transfixed the unwary customer.

As a boy in Australia, my friends and I collected snakes and spiders with all the curiosity of our age. We kept sticks with V-shaped ends to trap the ones we came across in the bush, and plonked empty paint tins over the poisonous funnel-web spiders that were encouraged to leave their holes in the ground. To us it was harmless fun, a hobby for the neighbourhood gang, and we tried to better each other by bringing back larger and larger specimens.

The father of one of my friends was horrified when he found out. The snakes were immediately released into the bush from the chicken-wire cages we constructed, but the spiders were unceremoniously introduced to the underside of a builder's shovel. Spiders, he said, were a menace. Snakes, on the other hand, kept the rat population down, even though they did on one occasion get the better of his cat.

The barber was proud of his collection of dead animals.

'You will have rats,' I warned.

He laughed without understanding why, then went back to his work, endlessly combing the hair of a man who had little left, as if that which remained should be flattered with every care and attention.

Nebi was next, and then I also was invited to take the chair, a classic barber's model in chrome and leather that reclined with some persuasion. At first I waved the offer away, but the barber was insistent. He pulled at my scraggy beard and hair and raised his eyebrows disapprovingly.

'You will look handsome for your family,' said Nebi from his seat by the door.

I smiled back at him and relented, sliding onto the padded leather seat that was torn in several places so that the foam showed through.

But when I looked straight ahead, the person in the mirror was someone I did not instantly recognise. Incredibly it was the first time I had seen my reflection in a long while. The Afghans carried their own tiny pocket mirrors for grooming, and none of the rooms I had stayed in lately were fitted with one. So it was for that reason I had gone on blissfully unaware of the changes that had occurred, changes that could not be detected so easily in the reflection of a passing shop window.

I looked younger, maybe not a kid again but certainly not thirty-nine at any rate. My face had thinned out and seemed longer, harder. My neck also the same, so that the muscles had grown quite apparent. What was most noticeable, however, were the eyes. The ones that stared back at me were sharp and bright. It was like looking at a photograph of someone I used to be, the one who used to wander across borders instead of boardrooms and whose office stretched to the horizon. It felt good to be back. Very good indeed.

'Nebi, I think I know the other reason I came back,' I called out.

But Nebi had already returned to his workshop, and the clatter of hammer on wood was sounding through the walls.

36

Deadlines are something we all must work to. My Afghan friend, my brother, had his. Mine was winging its way towards me at over eight hundred kilometres an hour, to pick me up like the magical white dove and return me to my own world. That moment, however, when I would have to say goodbye was not a sad one.

On the last day in Mashad, I rushed around to the Serai Sayid and shook the hands of Vali and Abdul, promising to return with busloads of tourists for them to 'cook'. Vali talked about business deals and carpets he could send for me to sell, and in truth the thought of becoming involved in his scheme was a tempting prospect, even if only as a side-line thing. But I also knew that I had other plans and goals, one of which was to gather all my notes and try and make sense of them in some kind of book.

In the end we agreed to write.

'Letters not e-mails,' he said as I descended the stairs. 'That bastard Arab down the road charges too much.'

From a pay phone near the shrine, where I waited in line behind the pilgrims, I dialled Jamal's mobile number and left a message of thanks when he failed to answer.

Finally, I caught a taxi to Nebi's house to gather my things in readiness for the night train back to Tehran. His wife had prepared some bread and fruit for which I was extremely grateful. In return, I left her with the contents of my medical kit: a bandage, a packet of Nurofen and some Imodium, none of which I had used.

I tried to explain what each was for, but then gave up and made her promise she would ask Ghollum Zabi to translate the instructions.

The children waved from the door, and I reserved a special hug for little Massoud. He hugged me back with his tiny arms and I immediately longed for the embrace of my own children. I was happy to be going, more so because I had done all that I came to do. Against so many odds, a hair-brained idea had become a not-so-hair-brained scheme after all – but a very important one.

Ghollum Zabi turned up and the three of us rode Nebi's bike to the train station as the late afternoon light began to fade. It was only a short distance and when we got there, the ticket collectors would not let them pass through to the other side where the train was waiting, so we had to say goodbye surrounded by a crowd of people.

Like the time before in the village of Seoshan, when he had left to return to the fighting, and I to my journey across the mountains to Pakistan, Nebi did not mince with words. He drew me to his chest, hugged me to both cheeks in the Afghan way and then stepped back. Ghollum Zabi did the same, though in his inimitable way he made a joke about the occasion, but it wasn't a very good one.

'Do you remember,' said Nebi, 'that I told you about my home in Herat? When you return, if we have gone from Mashad, it will be in this place that you will find us.'

'Where is it?' I asked.

'Beside the tomb of Gawhar Shad, under the afternoon shadow of the largest minaret.'

'The blue melon dome,' I said almost to myself, quoting Byron.

I turned to go and was about to pass through the gate when Nebi reached out and tapped my bag.

'I have left something in there for you,' he said.

'What is it?'

'You will see.'

But when I had passed through to the other side and boarded the train headed west, I opened the bag and looked. There was nothing there that I could see. Nothing at all.

37

It wasn't until I was in Dubai that I found his 'gift'. Waiting for my next flight, I decided to view a few of the digital video tapes to try and put them in some kind of order.

That was when I found his message. At some point he had set the camera on a shelf in the room where we slept, turned the screen around so that he could see himself, and then pressed the record button. What he had to say was no mere farewell. What he had to say was simply astonishing.

So this then, is Nebi's story, an Afghan's story.

My name is Ghollum Nebi Mohandaspoor.

[He pauses and shifts slightly to the right to place himself more in the middle of the picture. He is standing in the centre of the room with his arms to his side. The front door is behind him, slightly ajar. A strong light is coming through a rose-tinted window over his left shoulder, casting him in a strange hue.]

I am from Herat city in Afghanistan. I am thirty-eight and I have one wife, four children and five brothers: Abdul Khaliq, Abdul Ali, Qourban Ali, Aga Reza and Faheeq. I am the middle child.

Mister Richard, please excuse me for making this film, but it is the best way I think, to tell you something I have not told anyone for a long, long time. I hope you will find a translator in your country who can understand me.

When I was about the same age as my first son is now, my father told me there was going to be a war. He brought us to Mashad and he went to fight this war, but he did not come back.

[Long silence]

I was very angry.

[Long silence]

I could not understand why God had taken him. Why did God not punish the enemy and take them instead? I wanted to fight, but I was only a boy.

My oldest brother Abdul Khaliq went also, and for two years he fought against the Russians with the mujahedeen in western Herat. When he returned to us I was old enough to fight also, and I pleaded with him to take me back. I told him that I would find our father and rescue him from the enemy.

But they had hidden him; they put my father away in the dark places of Herat. I gave up all hope.

Then one day, you arrived out of nowhere and came with us to Afghanistan. At first I thought, what is this foreigner doing, what is the reason for him being here? But I could see you were a truthful man, and you looked so alone, so I decided to make sure no harm came to you. In time we became friends, and I learned many things about the world from you, and about the reasons for your journey, and how similar they were to mine. And it made me think, it made me hope again, of finding my own father.

The day after you left us, I went into the city at night. It was very dangerous, but with the Russians gone there was less risk than in the years before. I had also heard of a man who was a guard at the old Citadel of Pai Hesar. People paid him to find out what had happened to those who were captured or arrested, so I paid him to search the jails for my father. I waited in the shadows for many hours, until he finally returned with a man whom I did not recognise, such was his state. Both his legs were gone and he walked on wooden sticks. I can still remember the noise they made on the road.

[Pause]

His clothes were rags and his face in terrible pain. But Mister

Richard, it was the face of my father.

That night I held him in my arms. He was unconscious some of the time, but he knew it was me. I talked to him about the years we had looked for him, I told him I would carry him all the way to Mashad so that he could see his sons again, but they had broken his spirit as well as his body. He died before my eyes.

[Pause]

So you understand Mister Richard, you helped me as much as I helped you. I found my father and nursed him through his final hours, not in a lonely jail but with my arms around him. For that reason, in the name of God, I thank you.

Come back soon my friend. May Allah go with you.

I switched off the tape as the boarding call for my flight was announced. I felt a shiver go down my spine, a sense of my place in the world. A tiny shape in the puzzle into which I fitted. It was not a large piece, but it was a piece of the picture all the same.

38

The satellite phone rang with a distinctive sound, quite unlike an ordinary cellphone. Then there was a brief 'pip' of the call being answered, and a gruff man's voice speaking.

'*Belli.*'

'Ghollum Sefarr?' I asked.

Immediately the voice softened and reverted to English.

'Richard, is that you? I thought it was the office calling.'

He was shouting now with the excitement. 'You will never guess where I am. I am back in the Panshir with my rifle, hunting the ibex!'

I was about to say something about protected species when he burst in again. His words, however, were a jumble of squawks and clipped words as the satellite struggled to make a connection with this lone Afghan on a hilltop in Northern Afghanistan.

Then I heard him.

'She is walking!'

'What? Who is walking?'

'Hamid's sister. The one in the hospital. She said your friend did it. What was his name?'

'You mean Aziz!'

'That was the name, Doctor Aziz. She said he came in the night and told her that everything would be all right. He did nothing but sit with her and talk. Hamid told me this just two days ago when I was back in Herat. He is very happy, Richard.

Very, very happy. Can you hear me?'

'I can hear you Ghollum Sefarr, but I don't know what to say. It's incredible news.'

'Yes, yes! Incredible!'

It was either wind or static, but he suddenly sounded further away. Then his words turned into digitally muddled half-syllables and shortened vowels. I pictured him with his father's hunting rifle in one hand and the phone in the other, a part of the old world clutching something from the new, and the old world was winning. The satellite phone was being rejected from the body of this ancient land, until the soft electronic burr of a disconnected line signalled an end.

I placed the phone back on the table at home and looked outside at a garden that was full of the hectic, noisy life of children and the bright colour of spring flowers.

'Incredible,' I smiled. 'Absolutely bloody incredible.'

The author and the Afghan